# Letter to the White World

# Letter to the White World

**Alex Zanotelli**

Translated by Frank Stachyra

Orbis Books, the publishing arm of the Maryknoll Fathers and Brothers, endeavors to publish works that enlighten the mind, nourish the spirit, and challenge the conscience. To learn more about Maryknoll and Orbis Books, please visit our website at www.orbisbooks.com.

Copyright © Giangiacomo Feltrinelli Editore srl, Milano. First published as *Lettera alla tribù bianca* in "Serie Bianca" in March 2022.

English translation copyright © 2025 by Orbis Books.

Published by Orbis Books, Box 302, Maryknoll, NY 10545-0302.

In instances where original sources for foreign quotations could not be found, reasonable efforts have been made to provide an accurate translation. Any discrepancies or differences created in the translation are not binding and have no legal effect for compliance or enforcement purposes.

Scripture quotations are from The Revised Standard Version of the Bible, copyright © 1946, 1952, and 1971 National Council of the Churches of Christ in the United States of America. Used by permission. All rights reserved worldwide.

For quotations taken from Vatican documents, see www.vatican.va.

All rights reserved.

No part of this publication may be reproduced or transmitted in any form or by any means, electronic or mechanical, including photocopying, recording, or any information storage or retrieval system, without prior permission in writing from the publisher.

Queries regarding rights and permissions should be addressed to: Orbis Books, P.O. Box 302, Maryknoll, NY 10545-0302.

Manufactured in the United States of America.

---

Library of Congress Cataloging-in-Publication Data

Names: Zanotelli, Alex, author. | Stachyra, Frank, translator.
Title: Letter to the white world / Alex Zanotelli ; translated by Frank E. Stachyra.
Other titles: Lettera alla tribù bianca. English
Description: Maryknoll, New York : Orbis Books, [2025] | "Giangiacomo Feltrinelli Editore srl, Milano First published as Lettera alla tribù bianca in "Serie Bianca" in March 2022." | In English, translated from the original Italian. | Summary: "A lesson to the white world about the harm effected by racism, colonialism, and exploitation"— Provided by publisher.
Identifiers: LCCN 2024042728 (print) | LCCN 2024042729 (ebook) | ISBN 9781626986206 (trade paperback) | ISBN 9798888660751 (epub)
Subjects: LCSH: Race relations—Religious aspects—Christianity. | Racism—Religious aspects—Christianity. | White supremacy (Social structure)
Classification: LCC BT734.2 .Z36 2025 (print) | LCC BT734.2 (ebook) | DDC 277.30089—dc23/eng/20241207
LC record available at https://lccn.loc.gov/2024042728
LC ebook record available at https://lccn.loc.gov/2024042729

*To my teachers,*
*the slumdwellers of Korogocho*

# Contents

1. I Write to You . . .                                              9
2. In the World of the "Least"                                      13
   Coming out of the Cocoon    13
   Critical Reading    16
   At the School of the Impoverished    22
   Unveiling the Mystery    25
   Return to My Homeland    29
3. Hunger for Gold                                                  33
   Hunger for Gold    33
   Perverse Ideology    37
   Anthropological Poverty    40
   Systems of Terror    43
   Italians, Good People!    48
   The Theory of Race    50
4. White Supremacy                                                  55
   Injustice Built into the System    55
   A Disgraceful History    61
   The Complicity of the Churches    64
   The Epiphany of the White Supremacists    66
   The Genocide of the "Indians"    68

Latin America   72
Australia   74
Europe, the Homeland of the White Tribe   76
Italy: "State Racism"   81
"Lone Wolves"?   89

5. **Toward a Pluralistic Humanity**   95
Embarrassing Questions   95
A Cultural and Ethical Revolution   99
Reparations When?   106
And What of Contemporary Disasters?   110
And the Churches?   113

6. **A Contemporary Parable**   117
Coming out of the Colonial Cocoon   117
Pluralistic Humanity   120

7. **. . . To You, the Young**   125

# 1

# I Write to You . . .

These days the streets are silent. Gone is the usual melody that surrounds you and accompanies you in the Sanità District,[1] where I live in the bell tower of the church of Santa Maria: the honking of the mopeds passing you by as if on a carousel, voices of women talking from the balconies, shouts and laughing of children playing. . . . I, too, have had to halt everything for COVID-19.[2]

In obedience to the residents of Korogocho who sent me back to Europe, to my home country, Italy, to "convert it," I have taken advantage of the time to write this long letter to touch the hearts and the minds of you in the white world, who the residents of Korogocho, an impoverished community in Nairobi, Kenya, call the White Tribe. I carried back this

---

[1] Translator's note: A very poor section of Naples, Italy.

[2] Translator's note: Italy was the first Western country in which COVID-19 appeared, and its rapid spread overwhelmed its healthcare system nationwide with the gravely ill and quickly led to catastrophic numbers of deaths. As a result, the Italian government imposed a strict lockdown, prohibiting all activity but the most essential. Compliance was so complete as to virtually silence all Italian cities, including the normally raucous Piazza Sanità and its surroundings in Naples.

message and still carry in my very flesh the immense suffering of the people of Korogocho, along with that of the thousands of Korogochos of Africa—those shantytowns over the entire continent whose inhabitants now total two hundred million. The Korogochos are the bitter fruit of a perverse economic-financial system that, according to Pope Francis, produces "throwaways."

According to Oxfam, the richest 1 percent of the world's population, amounting to sixty-three million people, has emitted into the atmosphere twice as much carbon dioxide as the most impoverished half of the planet's population. It falls first of all to the white world—the White Tribe—to take concrete action to reverse this trend, but we continue in a lifestyle that is unsustainable for the earth. If all the peoples of the world lived as do the rich nations, we would need two or three planets. The egoism of the White Tribe is at the base of the environmental disaster that has menacing consequences for all humanity. Either we will be saved together or in the end we will all perish.

"The American way of life is not up for negotiation," declared President George H. W. Bush at the first Earth Summit in Rio de Janeiro (1992). But the ones who feel its most dramatic effects are precisely the impoverished peoples of the world. Not only do the rich countries continue a lifestyle that is unsustainable, but they also refuse to disburse the hundred billion dollars annually promised to the Global South so the impoverished might have aid to confront the ecological disasters brought on by us.

The consequence of the white world's actions will truly be an unmitigated growing exodus of migrants.

Our economic-financial-militarized system itself, in fact, creates ever more migrants: some flee hunger, some war, some climate disasters. According to the UN, which recognizes as refugees only those fleeing from war and from persecution, their total number is now at eighty-two million worldwide. Of these, a good 80 percent are from impoverished nations.

It is criminal that Europe, the United States, Canada, and Australia (who together make up the White Tribe) "welcome" those who are fleeing from hell with only walls, barbed wire, and police. It is inhuman to watch with indifference the thousands of dead in the Mediterranean, which has now become a Cimiterium Nostrum,[3] where tens of thousands of migrants are buried, lost in dreadful shipwrecks. I fear that posterity will say of us what we today say of the Nazis.

Is it possible that we have now lost empathy, the human quality that makes us feel the suffering of others as our own? How can we remain indifferent before the tragedies of refugees forced to live in the concentration camps of Libya or of the Greek isles? Or in the hell of those who control the "Balkan route" for those who wish to reach Europe?

When we turn our faces away from this dramatic scene, how can we still call ourselves human beings? Or worse: how can we still call ourselves Christians? This rejection of the "other," the impoverished and marginalized, underlies a latent racism that pervades the White Tribe. A racism, ridden by the extreme right, which today advocates the heresy of white supremacy that is corroding our very society.

We have witnessed the baptism of the white supremacist movement with the assault on the US Congress on January 6, 2021. Is the rapid expansion of the extremism of the right,

---

[3] Translator's note: *Cimiterium Nostrum*, Latin for "our cemetery," is a play on the name the ancient Romans gave to the Mediterranean Sea, because they had conquered virtually its entire perimeter, calling it *Mare Nostrum* ("our sea").

in Europe, in Italy too, perhaps an indicator of our lack of awareness of even belonging to the White Tribe, and of the fact that the period of our colonialism in Africa is over? When will we realize that we are part of a long history in which we have been, and continue to be, executioners?

We have a huge task before us, a mission that is all of ours, Christians and unbelievers alike: to see the "other" as a source of wealth for us, because they are different from us. Only in this way will we realize a pluralistic humanity; otherwise we are destined to tear each other apart. It is the dream of the "conviviality of differences," as my friend, Father Tonino Bello,[4] loved to call it. It is the dream of the "rainbow nation," that propelled Desmond Tutu to fight against apartheid in South Africa.

---

[4] Translator's note: Bishop Antonio Bello (1935–93) of Molfetta, a city on the southern Adriatic coast of Italy, was noted for his humility, declining the use of the honorific title for bishops in Italy (Monsignor), choosing, instead, to continue with that traditional for a parish priest (Don, or Father). Tonino is short for Antonio. As bishop, therefore, he was still Father Tony. The Catholic Church has opened the cause of his potential beatification; he was devoted to causes such as espoused in this book by Father Alex Zanotelli, including to that of the "least" of the world.

# 2

# In the World of the "Least"

## Coming out of the Cocoon

My life has been a sequence of fortuitous events as well as crises that have helped me radically rethink everything. As a boy I was fascinated by the figure of the missionary who risked his life for others. This fascination sprang from an encounter with a Comboni missionary[1] who came to speak in our school in Livo, a small town in the Val di Non, in Trentino, Italy,[2] where I was born; the story of his experience struck me to the core.

The Comboni missionaries provided me the opportunity to prepare well for such a path myself, including my studies in philosophy and theology, for eight long years, from 1956 to

---

[1] Translator's note: Comboni missionaries are a Roman Catholic religious order, named after its founder, St. Daniel Comboni, who devoted himself to the evangelization of Central, sub-Saharan Africa in the late 1800s. It has since expanded its work to many other areas in the world. Alex Zanotelli, a Catholic priest, is a member of that order.

[2] Translator's note: Trentino is a mountainous province of Italy, northwest of Venice.

1964, in the USA, at the theological school of Mt. St. Mary's, and at the Jesuit's Xavier University, both in Cincinnati, Ohio.

Those were the exhilarating years of Kennedy and the "New Frontier," of Martin Luther King Jr. It was also the era of the Second Vatican Council. In my studies I was introduced to the method of critical and scientific reading of the Bible, which, as a matter of religion, unsettled me profoundly. But above all I found myself smitten by America. Even Babylon could be seductive; the lifestyle of the American middle class of the 1960s was fascinating, and I was completely absorbed in it.

When I returned to Italy in 1964, it seemed I was landing on another planet. It was the Italy that was just rising again from the war, far from the United States in its, then, full economic boom.

In 1965 I was sent by my order to work in Sudan, to teach at the Comboni School of El-Obeid, a small city west of Khartoum, in the region of Kordofan, a large part of which was desert. The population there was 98 percent Muslim. For me the change of environments and the challenges were a shock. I prepared students, almost all Muslims, for the University of Khartoum. But I was unprepared to encounter the Islamic world. The culture that I had absorbed in my years of study in the USA was anti-Arab, anti-Islam, and prevented me from encountering the "other" I now taught: the Arab, the Muslim.

Initially overwhelmed, I had a strong desire to escape, but I remained at my post for eight years. Those years in Sudan, an impoverished country, helped me critically to reevaluate the USA and to understand that the wealth of the few is paid for by the misery of too many. I was really and truly shaken.

The experience helped me to comprehend just how much of the middle class culture I had absorbed in America. Greatly contributing to my being unsettled, too, while in this Arab milieu, was my closeness with the Nuba, one of the Black peoples suffering most in Africa in terms of persecution and oppression. In the city of El-Obeid, the Nuba were restricted to performing the most menial kinds of jobs. Fleeing from other regions of Africa, they had found refuge in the Nuba Mountains, in south Kordofan. And there they were then surrounded by Arab groups threatening to attack them to sell them as slaves.

The friendship that was born from working with so many of my Muslim students convinced me to study Arabic and Islam in depth. I was offered the opportunity of a two-year course at PISAI (Pontifical Institute of Arab and Islamic Studies of Rome). Those were two difficult years of intense study of Arabic, a language not easy to learn, yet fundamental for me because those years opened the door to another cultural and religious world.

I immersed myself in the study of the language, of the Qur'an, of the Arab world and history, culture, and great civilizations. I was, above all, fascinated by the mystical thread of Islam. When reading the writings of the greatest Islamic mystic, Al-Hallaj, I had the same impression as when reading the Spanish mystic St. John of the Cross: they were similar in the same passion for God, the same mystical doctrine of love.

Islam, in so many of its aspects, not only fascinated me but helped me to recover several elements of my own faith in God that I had neglected and ignored. This included, for example, the aspect—strongly emphasized in Islam—of God as totally *other*.

After these years of study I felt ready to return to Sudan for a serious dialogue with the Islamic world. But without any official explanation the government of Khartoum, headed by the dictator Nimeiry, denied me permission to reenter. It was 1975.

When many years later in Nairobi I met the head of the Nuba rebels, Yousif Kuwa, he revealed to me the reason for the denial: my closeness to his people, which to the government of Khartoum made me suspect of collusion with the Black peoples of southern Sudan, who were then in civil war against northern Sudan, in large part Arab and Islamic. And so I found myself staying in Italy, where the Comboni order asked me to take over the directorship of *Nigrizia*,[3] the order's magazine specializing in aspects of mission and culture in Africa. There I remained for nine long years. For me, working on the magazine was an extraordinary school for entry into the universe of the Black continent. A universe of which I was, in large part, ignorant.

## Critical Reading

Africa, birthplace of humanity, where *Homo Sapiens* first appeared, Africa of great civilizations and empires, the Africa of slavery and of colonialism, of the fight for liberation, for

---

[3] Translator's note: The word *nigrizia* does not appear in the Italian dictionary. It is based on the Latin word for "black," combined with an Italian ending, which would render it a noun signifying, roughly, "blackness." It corresponds to the French *nigritie*, which was in use by the 1700s to refer to a broad strip of sub-Saharan, central, interior Africa extending from the Nile westward nearly to the Atlantic. The term was used by St. Daniel Comboni in the mid 1800s to refer to his mission, and may here be understood to refer to Black Africa.

independence, land of neocolonialism, and neoliberalism. I was ignorant of the grave Western guilt with respect to this continent—for example, the crimes committed by Europeans—Italians—in the occupations of both Libya and Ethiopia.

In the course of reconstructing my outlook on Africa, I had to rethink everything. And I had to do the same concerning the mission and role of the church on the continent. And in the course of doing so I arrived at an awareness of a critical connection between colonialism and mission, and the unfortunate combination of colonization with the preaching of the gospel in Africa.

As director of *Nigrizia*, I supported the African churches in their effort to assimilate indigenous culture, to recover the values of traditional African religion, above all in the liturgical and theological fields. This long and difficult process includes the need to reformulate Christian theology, rethink faith as a given, beginning with Greek thought, to terms consonant with African culture and philosophy. So I supported the theology of assimilation and the *Black theology* of the Black communities in the fight against apartheid in South Africa.

The theologies of assimilation sought to reinterpret not only Western theology in terms of African thought, but also the liturgy of the Latin Church, in liturgies closer to the African spirit, as happened in Zaire (now the Democratic Republic of Congo) with the Zaire Rite of the Eucharist.

All this brought us to a confrontation with the Vatican in the person of then Cardinal Ratzinger (who years later would become pope), as he requested a retraction of some errors regarding Catholic doctrine contained in a *Nigrizia* article by the Cameroonian theologian Meinrad Hebga. "The ideological and cultural monopoly of the Gospel of Jesus on the part of the West," wrote Hebga, "becomes more intolerable in the moral sphere, when one sees certain men profit from their position of authority in the Church to impose on all nations, in the name of God, the ethical sensibility proper to their own cultural area."

*Nigrizia* also supported all the theologies of the Global South: Latin American liberation theology, the theology of Indigenous peoples of South America, Black theology of the Black churches in the USA, and the various theologies of Asia. For us at *Nigrizia* it was important to host the voices of the theologians of Africa and the Global South because we were opposed to the cultural imperialism of the Western church, which imposed on the churches of the South a single theology, a single liturgy—Roman—and a single canon law.

The critical approach taken by *Nigrizia* also could not help but offer a serious analysis of Italian governmental policy toward Africa. Above all because, from investigative reporting, all the misdeeds were emerging from a so-called Italian "cooperation" with the Black continent.

It was in the 1980s that a great Italian campaign was launched against hunger in Africa, promoted by radicals, manipulated by the Socialists of Craxi, and finally blessed by the Christian Democratic Party of Piccoli. The reality underlying so many obscure points of that campaign became clear. Both Craxi and Piccoli were acting within the "Italian campaign," which I tried to summarize in the editorial "The Italian Face of African Hunger" (*Nigrizia*, January 1985). This foreshadowed a far broader national scandal that would afterward become known as Tangentopoli,[4] the incredible interweaving of business and politics. The editorial became a national sensation, triggering a huge political debate in all of Italy's daily papers, but above all, among the political parties making up the Government.

After a careful analysis of the proposed law that pledged the Italian government's serious fight against hunger in Africa, the editorial concluded with this scathing analysis: "The more we analyze this matter of aid to the countries of Africa," I wrote, "the more we are convinced that it primarily serves our benefit, and then that of the elite middle class of the impoverished countries, to maintain themselves in power. And so the 'system' continues to turn."

A veritable pandemonium broke out, with a slew of threats of lawsuits. I felt like a flea at the mercy of enormous powers. I often anxiously wondered: "Is it possible that fifty million Italians don't see what is happening? Am I sure that what I wrote is the truth?" I am convinced that no one possesses the truth, but that a person can arrive at the truth through a serious encounter with anyone who holds a different perspective. I am also convinced that this entire economic system of ours is based on a lie, and its first victim is the truth.

Out of that controversy over aid and hunger there came to light a further close connection: one between hunger and military armaments. I wondered: "How is it possible that with one hand Italy offers aid, and, in turn, with the other,

---

[4] Translator's note: Tangentopoli (or Bribesville) was an Italian national political scandal of a period a few years later, in the early 1990s, involving the extensive bribery of many public officials by widespread Italian economic interests.

sells weapons?" Those years witnessed a quite real Italian boom in the production and exportation of arms. We faced an issue that the magazine could not be silent about, when the situation urgently called for a clear, precise response. A serious look at the subject of armaments grew from that, as concerns were shared by many committed laymen and laywomen of the church in Northeast Italy,[5] as together with them we issued the document *Blessed Are the Peacemakers*, in which we asked Christians and citizens to object to the financing of military expenditures. The document concluded by asking the Christian community to make these important pledges:

- to be bearers of the prophetic message of peace, by conscientious objection to: military service and scientific research related to the production of, and commerce in, armaments; to invoke the "tax objection"[6]; to achieve the denuclearization of the national territories;
- to invoke conscientious objection to working in arms production; and to support the conversion of the nation's existing arms factories to peaceful uses;
- to push for the abolition of military secrecy regarding commerce in armaments;

---

[5] Translator's note: Specifically, Triveneto, a large area comprising the broad territory surrounding Venice.

[6] Translator's note: The "tax objection" was an organized form of civil disobedience, by which citizens deducted a percentage of their tax bill destined for the Ministry of Defense and sent it, instead, to a foundation for peace.

- to denounce and oppose all mass weapons of extermination (atomic, biological, and chemical);
- to choose nonviolence as the means to achieve the citizens' right/duty of defense (a people's nonviolent defense).

The bishops in the region immediately signed the document. And immediately it unleashed a political and ecclesiastical storm. Giovanni Spadolini, then national minister of defense, attacked the "red priests" who, in his opinion, were threatening the security of the country. The Vatican secretary of state immediately intervened, calling on the bishops of Triveneto to retract their signatures from the document. And, unfortunately, they obeyed.

But we were not intimidated by Spadolini. In collaboration with two other missionary magazines, I penned a new, urgent editorial in which we declared Spadolini to be "a salesman of the instruments of war." Again, the response was not long in coming: "The declarations of the Director of *Nigrizia* constitute an incitement to international criminal terrorism." Spadolini, together with the Italian minister of foreign affairs, Giulio Andreotti,[7] placed great pressures on the Vatican to get me dismissed from my role as director.

---

[7] Translator's note: Giulio Andreotti would be well known to Zanotelli's Italian readers. He was a long-time Italian political figure, and, at the time, the Italian minister of foreign affairs; he had also been previously, and was afterward, for a total of seven times, the Italian prime minister. He would be all the more well known, as he was also convicted, in 2002, of conspiracy to commit murder for ordering the death of a journalist in 1979, and sentenced to twenty-four years. The conviction was later overturned on appeal as coming too late, that is, beyond the statute of limitations.

It is not easy to feel the weight on one's shoulders of betrayal by one's own church and of one's own religious family, but that is what happened. To speak the truth in the face of power is an act of courage for which one must pay. I was "torpedoed" as the director of *Nigrizia*. To refuse to retreat when faced down by power, to keep affirming the truth that emerges from the reality of facts, to use the weight of clear denunciation on the printed page: these must all be paid for. I know this well. Still, I will not hide a distinct bitterness over that banishment, not for myself, but for the effects on the extraordinary movement that had been in formation.

## At the School of the Impoverished

All events, including unhappy ones, carry with them a potential opportunity. For a long time I had already been considering a return to Africa to live among those in the shanties, to feel on my own skin the suffering of the least. So it was that in 1988 I arrived at Nairobi, the capital of Kenya. Nairobi is a city of four million inhabitants, a splendid metropolis with palatial buildings and skyscrapers in its downtown, but it is surrounded by immense shantytowns, where 70 percent of the population lives, called shanty people.

I recall the first time I celebrated the Eucharist in a parish in the shantytowns. Right at the start of the celebration, I asked the faithful willing to come to the altar to trace the sign of the cross on my palms, offering the words: "I forgive you, white brother"! Immediately as I arrived in the Black continent I felt the deep need to seek pardon for all the evil that my White Tribe had done to the Black peoples.

It was my wish to live in one of the many shantytowns that encircle Nairobi, but no missionary had ever done it. How could a white missionary choose to move to a place like that? Deep opposition was stirred up against my desire, a general opposition, but one that centered in the will of the Cardinal of Nairobi.

After two years of waiting, I arrived at the shantytown of Korogocho,[8] considered then the most violent of the city and also one of the most destitute. On January 14, 1990, I left the Youth Center, where I was living, and, knapsack on my back, I walked through Korogocho. It was my "descent into the underworld." It was the Sunday of the Baptism of Jesus and I celebrated the Eucharist with the few Christians there. I explained to them in my poor Kiswahili (the official language of Kenya) that I had chosen that day, precisely, because I felt the need to be "baptized" by them. I felt that I was a petit-bourgeois that needed the baptism of the impoverished. I chose to live as they did, to eat what they ate, to go as they do, to buy my water with a tank, to live their daily life, often violent and dramatic. I quickly ditched the forty-five pounds that we Westerners accumulate.

More than anything else, the human horrors I encountered drove me mad. So many times I was overtaken with a deep discomfort, with the wish to bash my head against the wall of the shanty. In that immense extension of sheet metal that is

---

[8] Translator's note: *Korogocho* is a Swahili word signifying (according to multiple sources) "crowded shoulder to shoulder." Although it is often described simply as a "slum," Zanotelli refers to it with an Italian word that is a combination of one for a shack, or shanty, plus one signifying city or town, i.e., translated, a "shantytown."

Korogocho, the absurdity of our world was made plain. From the holes in my shanty I could see the skyscrapers of Nairobi; and at only 2.5 miles from Korogocho lies Muthaiga, the most beautiful and luxurious residential zone of the metropolis, with its dreamlike villas. Nairobi is a city in which, within the space of a few miles, you pass from paradise to hell. Or rather, into the underworld.

There are so many of these "underworlds" in that area! The worst, perhaps, rises at the edge of the shantytown: the enormous and fearful garbage dump of Dandora, where the refuse from the rich of the capital winds up, or to be precise, the refuse of the refuse; that is, what's left of it after the thousands of garbage pickers who work there (called scavengers) have finished with it.

One day, while I was walking among the shanties of Korogocho, I was blocked by one of the men from the Dandora dump, a "giant" who looked down at me from above: "*Muthungu*" (white man), he said to me, "you are the first white who has had the courage to live *here*." I answered: "I have just arrived *here*; but you're right! Tomorrow, I'll be *there*, with *you*."

That night a delegation of Christians came to meet me. They were visibly worried: "Father, we heard that tomorrow you want to go into the dump. You can't go there; those are criminals. They will kill you." I stayed silent for a few moments, reflecting on those words. "I did not come to Korogocho on account of saints," I answered, "but for the criminals."

The next day I took up my knapsack and started walking. Once I arrived at the top of a hill, I was met by a flock of vultures, and spread out before me was an infernal specter: an immense lowland with mountains of trash, fires everywhere, hundreds of scavengers: men and women of all ages, from the very old to very young children. I felt a terror overcome me; my first instinct was to run away. By happenstance, I saw that giant who had challenged me to go to the dump, Jeremias. I ran up to him, almost as if to seek protection. When he saw me, he looked at me with an ironic smile: "*Muthungu*, I did not think you whites would keep your promises!"

He sat me down on a pile of filth and began to explain to me the dump's system: everything is controlled by a network of mafiosi. I saw the trucks arrive and unload, and then dozens and dozens of people fighting each other to get hold of the most garbage possible, to then resell it in order to earn a living. Still traumatized, I looked at Jeremias, with his good-natured attitude, who invited me to follow him to greet his people. So many handshakes, the first smiles. It was the beginning of what would be, eventually, a long walk to enter into that world: the world of the least.

My choice at Korogocho was precisely the world of the "throwaways": the garbage pickers, the boys and the girls of the street, the bands of petty thieves, the many sick with AIDS, and the very youngest girls, who headed into the city as prostitutes.

And it was particularly those girls who most affected my response to that place.

## Unveiling the Mystery

When I would go out early in the morning to buy a little bread, I would encounter them returning from the city. I often invited them into my shanty to have some tea. It was a chance to talk to them, informing them of the risk of contracting

AIDS in their work. "You don't have to tell us that," they responded, a little irritated. "We know it; we will all die of AIDS." I recall particularly well when a girl said to me: "Alex, take a sheet of paper and write my name: 'Njeri Njoki, died of AIDS.' Then on another sheet write: 'Njeri Njoki, died of hunger.' Roll up each of those two pieces of paper and then pick one out and read it aloud." But before I finished doing it, she stopped me: "Do you know which of the two is the paper where you wrote 'died of AIDS'? Give it to me," she said. "At least I will live a few more years."

I wished I could have sunk into the earth: I felt like a worm. I, as a priest, would have myself be pure, chaste, the man of God who can celebrate the Eucharist and eat of his Jesus. They? No. They are prostitutes. What's more, I thought to myself, I am a *white* priest, part of an economic-financial system that creates this planet of shantytowns and that obliges these girls to prostitute themselves to be able to survive! All the moral theology that I had been taught crumbled completely in the face of their stories. I seemed no longer able to comprehend; I understood nothing.

Yet it was these very girls who bestowed on me such incredible access to the Mysteries that surround us.

I will relate just one very meaningful example: one evening two people came to my shanty to tell me that a girl, Florence, was very ill. Every evening I used to go to celebrate the Eucharist in the shanties of those who were ill with AIDS, along with the small community in the place. I promised that I would go immediately, and, accompanied by two other priests, I came to her. Florence had been forced at the age of eleven into the path of prostitution by her mother, who needed money; at fifteen she had been diagnosed with AIDS.

It was already night when I arrived at her shanty; she didn't know I was coming. I knocked. I heard a feeble little voice: "*Karibu!*" (Welcome!). I opened the door. And, although it was pitch dark, I said, "Florence, *jambo*?" (how are you?). She answered: "Oh, it's you, Alex! How wonderful!" I slowly entered, feeling my way through the dark. Then I glimpsed her, spread out on her little bed. She was very ill. I approached, and I told her, "Florence, would you light this candle so we can see?" She lit it. And her face appeared—a very beautiful face, but now deformed by pustules. "Do you want to pray, Florence?" I whispered to her, and she, with the candle in her hand, began a prayer of poignant beauty. On my death bed I will never succeed in saying a prayer so beautiful. When she finished, I asked her, "Florence, who is God for you?"

"*Mungu, ni mama*" (God is Mamma), was her reply, leaving me astonished. Florence was dying, alone, at age sixteen, in a shanty, while her own mother had abandoned her a few days earlier.

I summoned all my courage and asked her, "But then, who is the face of God for you today?" She sunk down in a silence that seemed would never end. I had my eyes fixed on her face, when she suddenly blossomed into a very beautiful smile: "I am the face of God." And then we celebrated the Eucharist together.

It is extraordinary to see the spirituality of the impoverished in such tragic moments. Their faith, their serenity, and their capacity to express Mystery. God does exist, but God is found in the hell of the least. He is not the omnipotent God who solves everything with "little miracles"; he is the tender, weak God who walks with the "throwaways" of humanity, who cries with them.

The silence of God, however, obliges us to take our responsibilities in hand, to leave behind our expectations of miracles, and enter the road of personal, social, economic, and political engagement we are called to. Few have expressed this so well as Etty Hillesum, a young Jewish writer, deported and cremated at Auschwitz: "But one thing," she wrote in her diary,[9] "is becoming increasingly clear to me: that You [God] cannot help us, that we must help You to help ourselves."[10]

It was the impoverished who not only helped me penetrate the Mystery that surrounds us, but who also helped me to reread the Bible with other eyes. To discover the God who feels the suffering inflicted on the oppressed and comes down to free them. But he does it by Moses, or, today, through Desmond Tutu, Nelson Mandela, Martin Luther King Jr. . . . This is the theology of liberation, the Black theology of South Africa under apartheid, as is also that of Black Americans, so well expressed by James Cone in his book *The Cross and the Lynching Tree*. Desmond Tutu, the Anglican archbishop who fought against apartheid, writes in *God Has a Dream*: "God will come, because he has a Dream, and it will be realized through us. Because we are his collaborators. We have been chosen to liberate the oppressed. . . . And it is thus that we shall dry the tears on the face of God."

---

[9] Translator's note: Alex Zanotelli, who is a polyglot fluent in English, quotes in Italian a number of authors who actually wrote in English, or whose work has already been translated into a published English version. Whenever such a source is readily available in English, this work quotes it directly.

[10] Etty Hillesum, *Etty, The Letters and Diaries of Etty Hillesum 1941–1943*, complete and unabridged, ed. Klaas A. D. Smelik, trans, Arnold J. Pomerans (Grand Rapids, MI: Eerdmans, 2002), 488.

## Return to My Homeland

It was this spirituality of the oppressed that gave me the strength to carry on the fight for twelve years, at the side of the people of the shantytown of Korogocho and the other shantytowns of Nairobi. Above all was the fight for the land, because the ground where the shantytowns arise is not the property of the people who live there, but of the government. And we in the community were asking the government of Kenya to entrust the land to the entire population of the shantytowns in what we called a "land community trust."

The night before I departed Korogocho, the heads of the small communities and the pastors of the various independent churches of the shantytowns came to tell me that I could not leave Korogocho before they had prayed over me, and for me. I was quite delighted with that.

That night so many of us met together, in a very intense prayer that lasted over two hours. At the end, one of them said to me: "Alex, get down on your knees!" I got down on my knees in the midst of them.

Another said: "Place your hands on him." I felt what seemed like hundreds of hands on my head and body. And a pastor of an independent African church, the reverend Timothy, began to pray charismatically. "Father, thank you that Alex has walked with us at Korogocho for twelve years." And he continued, recalling so many beautiful and difficult moments lived together with the various churches and with the Muslims of Korogocho. And he concluded his long prayer crying out: "Father, now Father Alex will return to his own people. I pray you, Father, give Father Alex your Holy Spirit." And those present, with their hands on my head, squashed me to the ground to make me feel the force of the Spirit. "Give him your Spirit, with power, so that now he may return to *his white tribe, and convert it!*"

The people of the shantytowns were now sending me back to convert my own White Tribe, because, if we live today on a planet of immense masses of the impoverished, the responsibility in great part is on the White Tribe. And as a missionary I have returned to my people, to my White Tribe to "convert it."

Having returned to Italy, I chose to live in the South, the most depressed region of the country, and specifically Naples, the largest metropolitan area of the South, with its grave social problems. In the city of Naples I chose to live in the near periphery of the city, in the Sanità District. For a missionary it is fundamental to be in that area in order to hear the cry of suffering of the "throwaways" and see reality with other eyes.

From where I live it is unbelievable to see the distance that divides the "well-off Naples" (Chiaia, Posillipo, Vomero), from the "poor Naples" (including the far periphery districts, from Scampia to Ponticelli, to those more near, from the Spanish Quarter to the Sanità District). Two worlds that do not see each other and do not speak to each other.

I am part of a small missionary community that lives in simplicity and in small lodgings in the bell tower of the church of Santa Maria of Sanità. Living with me are Father Arcadio Sicher, a Franciscan who has worked in the shantytowns of Africa; and a consecrated lay person, a retired pediatrician, Felicetta Parisi. We are engaged in giving a hand to this district with grave social problems, but also to the least of the metropolis: the homeless, migrants, the Roma, and others. The economic-financial system creates the impoverished of the Global South, but in the rich countries, too, it creates the "throwaways," the "refuse," as Pope Francis says.

And from here, obedient to the people of the shantytown of Korogocho who have sent me to convert "my White Tribe," I would like to issue a message that speaks to the heart so that it will convert. Mine is not an act of accusation; it is a humble attempt, as a missionary, to help the White Tribe change course. I need a life of encounters with the "other" to understand what it means to be white and how the "other" sees us. I am well aware that for us whites to emerge from the cocoon to encounter the "other" is not easy. I know how difficult it has been for me. So it is with great humility that I address this message to the White Tribe so that it will convert. To convert, in the Bible, means to "change course," calling on anyone and everyone on the wrong path.

You may ask me why the Africans of Korogocho classify us as the White Tribe. Just as we whites have always referred to the peoples of Black Africa as belonging to "tribes," in a derogatory sense, the Africans define us Europeans as the White Tribe.

But why do the Hausa peoples of Nigeria, who are eighty million in number, have to be called a tribe, while the Swiss, who are less than eight million, are a people? We must carefully analyze our terminology in describing the "other": today we call the impoverished countries "developing nations," using language that the liberation theologian Jon Sobrino defines as "euphemistic and macabre." Are we truly sure that it is we who are the developed and civilized countries?

I turn then to White Europe, which defines itself as Christian, to ask it if it has ever truly been so. The noted psychoanalyst Eric Fromm, in his book *To Have or To Be?*, posed the same question and answered it, saying that Europe has only been painted with Christianity, but its foundations have remained profoundly pagan. Today this is more than evident. Pope Francis, with great courage in his 2019 Christmas message, said that we are not within Christianity—not anymore.

# 3

# Hunger for Gold

## Hunger for Gold

How can Europe call itself Christian—that is, followers of Jesus, who taught the way of love and of nonviolence—when the white world that conquered and colonized the world in the name of Christ was motivated by hunger for gold?

The story begins with those first imperial powers, Spain and Portugal, followed by England, Holland, France, Germany, Belgium, and Italy. The White Tribe colonized the world believing itself to be possessed of *civilization, culture,* and *religion,* assumptions making us feel entitled to conquer the world in the name of God. The White Tribe felt itself duty bound to colonize the world, to bring Christian civilization to the so-called barbarians. It has believed that for centuries. These are the deep roots of white supremacy and of racism. These are the foundations on which the European powers conquered and colonized the world, with all the horrors that followed.

It was Spain that began this process with the so-called discovery of America (1492). By what right did Spain build its immense empire, conquering all (except Brazil) of Central and South America? Nothing but that of the *superiority of its own civilization, culture, and religion.*

"Conquistadors, and those endowed with grants of Indian forced labor, plus the theologians who supported them," states Peruvian liberation theologian Gustavo Gutiérrez, in his study *Dios O El Oro En Las Indias (God or Gold in the Indies),*

> were full of themselves in their presumed human superiority, in the world of their homeland, and in their search for the precious metal. In their vision the Indians had no value of their own (they were a *tabula rasa*,[1] as Columbus had once declared!). Their destiny was to work for those who had newly arrived and eventually to become like them. That mentality was well illustrated, for example, in the almost obsessive undertaking of giving new names to all that they encountered, both things and people. The very term *Indians* proved to be an erroneous name with which to label the inhabitants of this continent; in practice, they seemed nonentities.

Europe considers itself the center of the world; its experience of the "other" is the other as dominated. "I mean by *invention* [of the Americas] Columbus's construing of the islands he encountered as Asian. . . . As a result, the Other, the American 'Indian,' disappeared," affirms the Argentine philosopher Enrique Dussel in his study *The Eclipse of the Other.* "This Indian was not discovered as Other, but subsumed under categories of the Same. This Indian was known beforehand, as Asiatic, and re-known in the face-to-face encounter, and so denied as Other, or *covered over (en-*

---

[1] Translator's note: *Tabula rasa* is Latin for "an erased writing tablet," that is, a blank slate or something on which anything could be written.

*cubierto)*." It was on this basis that the "conquest" of the Aztec lands began, of the Maya, and the Incas, homicidal wars, with fearful massacres. The Indians were forced to work on the farms of the Spaniards but, above all, in the mines.

The Spaniards were hungry for gold. "The mine's mouth represents metaphorically the mouth of Moloch requiring human sacrifice—a sacrifice not to the bloody Aztec god," continues Dussel, "but to the invisible god Capital, the new deity of occidental, Christian civilization." The result was the appalling decline of the native population, whether by wars, by forced labor, or by diseases, such as smallpox, or measles, to which the Indigenous population had no immunity. In Peru it appears that the population may have decreased from nine million in 1520 to one million in 1570.

I will not review here all that happened in that era. I address only its significance, also well expressed by Dussel: "In this violent relationship the conqueror was pitted against the conquered; advanced military technology against an underdeveloped one. At this beginning of modernity, the European ego experienced a quasi-divine superiority over the primitive, rustic, inferior Other. The modern ego [was] covetous of wealth, power, and glory."

No less violent was the meeting of the two spiritual worlds: that of the Europeans, and that of the Indigenous peoples. At this level we cannot overlook that the Borgia pope, Alexander VI, had issued a pontifical bull in which he granted ownership of the newly discovered islands to King Ferdinand and Queen Isabella of Spain.[2] The conquest was understood

---

[2] Translator's note: Pope Alexander VI was a member of the Borgia family of the kingdom of Aragon, ruled by Ferdinand of Aragon, who was also the husband of Queen Isabella of Castile. On May 4, 1493, just nine

to be based on a divine plan. The conquistadors called out the native people, before attacking them in battle, to convert to Christianity: "I require you to recognize the church as queen and superior of the world, to acknowledge the pope in the church's name, and to obey his majesty, the pope's vicar, who is superior, lord, and king of these lands."

The religion of the native peoples was, therefore, the work of the devil as that of the whites was divine. "They interpreted the Other's world as negative, pagan, satanic, and intrinsically perverse," writes Dussel. "Since the Spanish considered indigenous religion demonic and theirs divine, they pursued a policy of tabula rasa, the complete elimination of indigenous beliefs, as a first step in replacing those beliefs with their own."

There was, however, even among the conquerors, a prophetic church inspired by the Dominican friars guided by Bartholomè de las Casas (1484–1566), the bishop of Chiapas, Mexico. He led a life that brought him to discover the Indigenous "other" as different from Western civilization. Aware of the gravity of the situation, the Dominican friars endorsed a sermon preached by Friar Antonio De Montesinos on the fourth Sunday of Advent in 1511:

> You are all in mortal sin; you live in it and will die in it, for the cruelty and tyranny that you practice with these innocent people. Tell me, with what right and with

---

months after his elevation as pope, and just two months after the return of Columbus from his first voyage of discovery, he issued a papal bull, *Inter Caetera,* awarding all of the islands Columbus had discovered, plus all the mainlands to their west (i.e., virtually the entire Western Hemisphere), to Ferdinand and Isabella, who were jointly ruling what would become modern Spain.

what justice do you hold these Indians in such cruel and horrible servitude? With what authority have you waged such detestable wars on these peoples who were so meek and peaceful in their own lands, where you have destroyed so many, an infinity of them, with death and massacres? Are not they men, these? Do they not have rational souls? Are you not obliged to love them as yourselves?

## Perverse Ideology

That which Spain did in the Americas, the Portuguese did in Africa, beginning as early as 1415 with the conquest of Ceuta (Morocco). In 1471 the Portuguese reached the Gold Coast (today's Ghana) where they created the Elmina Fortress, procuring gold and African slaves in exchange for European goods.

Later, with the voyage of Vasco da Gama (1497), they circumnavigated Africa to arrive at India (1498). The decisive factor that allowed Portugal, a small country, to extend its rule from Africa to the "Indies" (now the islands of Southeast Asia) was the support of the powerful European groups that financed the several expeditions. So it was that Lisbon also constructed an enormous colonial empire. Here too, as in the Americas, there was no meeting with the peoples of Africa. Instead, the Portuguese were the first to capture and sell Africans as slaves. This first encounter between "Christian" European and "pagan" Africa was devastating.

But the Portuguese were soon enough displaced by another seafaring power, Holland, which built a colonial empire ranging from South Africa to Indonesia. Then it was the turn of two great European powers, England and France, to build two more enormous colonial empires, practically dividing the Global South between them. England took possession (besides North America), of Australia, India, and southern Africa (South Africa and Rhodesia); France took a large part of North and Central Africa.

It was in this setting that the transatlantic African slave trade expanded exponentially, with the "Great Circle" of commerce (which actually took triangular form). Already in 1518 the King of Spain had granted Governor Lorenzo de Gomenot the license to send four thousand slaves to Haiti and Jamaica "directly from the islands of Guinea and other regions from which the taking of said Negroes is customary." After that, besides Spain, the other European colonial powers, especially Holland, England, and France, who were colonizing the new lands in the Americas, increasingly also participated in the slave trade. With every new sugar plantation or gold mine, there was a new shipment of slaves.

It has been calculated that ten to twenty million African slaves were transported to the Americas: millions of Africans, pulled up from their roots, dragged in chains to another continent where their lives were consumed in the hard labor of the plantations and mines. It is one of the most shameful pages of human history, which has been emblazoned on the souls of Africans. It is the great misunderstood Holocaust of human history, and it is at the foundation of the great wealth of the white world.

French historian Abbé Alphonse Quenum, who has devoted an important study to the trade, *Les Églises chrétiennes et la traite atlantique du XV$^e$ au XIX$^e$ siècle*, speaks of an "astounding silence" on the part of the church. Its first condemnation of the trade, according to Quenum, came only with Pope Gregory XVI in 1839. It is another of the historic sins of the church.

That is why African American theologian Ebony Marshall Turman of Yale, in an important meeting of students of religions, asserted that "White Christianity in America was born in heresy." To understand such an assertion, American Christian ethicist David P. Gushee in his 2020 September/October *Sojourners* article "White American Christianity Is Rooted in Colonial Empire-Building," states, "A compelling starting point is 15th century Europe as it began conquering and colonizing the world in the name of Christ."

These nations who built vast colonial empires, Gushee writes, "confidently believed themselves to be the center of the world, superior to all other cultures, entitled to conquer and colonize, and in doing so actively advancing God's will. The European powers believed this for many centuries." And he adds that they believed

> they were the best people on earth, the most advanced, the agents of civilization, the bearers of faith. Their church told them that they had the right and duty to conquer, colonize, extract, and even enslave entire non-European populations.... They were also better because they were persons of the "race" and "color" called "white," by contrast with lesser persons of other colors and races.

Gushee concludes: "The single best term to describe this kind of vision is white supremacism."

This perverse ideology brought about the extermination of the Indigenous peoples of North America and the confinement of the survivors in "reservations." In the USA, this is the original sin, followed thereafter by the enslavement of millions of Africans, treated like animals, without any rights: beasts of burden for work on the cotton plantations. The enslaved lived under the terror of the whip and of lynching. "White theologians in the past century," writes the noted Afro-American theologian James Cone in his masterpiece *The Cross and the Lynching Tree*,

> have written thousands of books about Jesus' cross without remarking on the analogy between the crucifixion of Jesus and the lynching of black people. One must suppose that in order to feel comfortable in the Christian faith, whites needed theologians to interpret the gospel in a way that would not require them to acknowledge white supremacy as America's great sin. Churches, seminaries, and theological academies separated Christian identity from the horrendous violence committed against black people. Whites could claim a Christian identity without feeling the need to oppose slavery, segregation, and lynching as a contradiction of the gospel for America.

## Anthropological Poverty

The slave trade was eventually abolished at the beginning of the 1800s, thanks to many humanitarian movements, but above all because it did not answer any longer to the economic interests of industrial capitalism, which required, instead, new forms of "lawful" commerce. And so came the transformation of Africa from the supplier of slaves to the supplier of raw materials. The era of colonization then began, with the eventual seal of approval of the Berlin Conference (1884–85), which sanctioned "spheres of influence" under the doctrine of actual occupation: the country that controlled the coastal zone had the right to possess the entire interior. The partitioning of Africa occurred at this conference.

European colonialism on that continent was extremely heavy and truly a looting of the raw materials used to enrich Europe, while Africa went into ever-growing impoverishment, even with its richness of natural resources. But the deepest damage was psychological. Noted Cameroonian theologian Engelbert Mveng, who was assassinated at his home in Yaounde—generating a suspicion it was by the current regime—called it "anthropological poverty," the bitter fruit of slavery and colonialism.

"The brutal stampede out of Europe," writes the Cameroonian philosopher Achille Mbembe in his study *Critique of Black Reason*,

> came to be known as *colonization* or *imperialism*. Colonization was one of the central mechanisms through which the European pretension of universal domination was made manifest. It was a form of constitutive power whose relationship to land, populations, and territory brought together the three logics of race, bureaucracy, and commerce (*commercium*) in a way that was new in the history of humanity.

He continues:

> The plantation and colonial systems were the factories par excellence of race and racism. The "poor Whites" in particular depended on cultivating differences that separated them from Blacks to give themselves the sense of being human. The racist subject sees the humanity in himself not by accounting for what makes him similar to others but by accounting for what makes him different. . . . As a slave, the Black Man represents one of the troubling figures of our modernity, and in fact constitutes its realm of shadow, of mystery, of scandal. As a human whose name is disdained, whose power of descent and generation has been foiled, whose face is disfigured, and whose work is stolen, he bears witness to a mutilated humanity, one deeply scarred by iron and alienation.

Mbembe concludes with these weighty words for the era in which we live: "We cannot act as if slavery and colonization never took place, or as if we are completely rid of the legacies of such an unhappy period."

In their entirety, those legacies are still the poisonous fruit of a racist European ideology as expressed at the beginning of the nineteenth century by one of the most famous European philosophers, Georg Wilhelm Friedrich Hegel, in *Lectures on the Philosophy of History*:

> In Negro life the characteristic point is the fact that consciousness has not yet attained to the realization of any substantial objective existence, for example, God, or Law. . . . The Negro, as already observed, exhibits the natural man in his completely wild and untamed

state. . . . At this point we leave Africa, not to mention it again. For it is no historical part of the World; it has no movement or development to exhibit. . . . What we properly understand by Africa, is the Unhistorical, Undeveloped Spirit, still involved in the conditions of mere nature, and which had to be presented here only as on the threshold of the World's History.

Hegel's is one of the most repulsive and shameful pages in all of philosophy, and his work expresses, better than any other text, the true nature of European racism that led to slavery and to colonialism.

I will not enter here into the European colonial venture in Africa in detail; the English, French, Dutch, and Portuguese colonialism in the African continent would require volumes. I will only include below a few reference points: to French colonialism in Algeria; to English colonialism in South Africa; and then, to what is less well known, that of the last three European nations that turned toward Africa: Belgium, Germany, and Italy.

## Systems of Terror

The true face of French colonialism revealed itself in Algeria, where a million French colonists settled, dominating every aspect of life of the country. Paris considered Algeria to be French territory, with the most fertile lands owned by the French. In 1945 the first popular uprising led to the killing of some one hundred colonists. France reacted with indescribable brutality, killing at least forty-five thousand Algerians. This began the armed struggle of the Algerian people against the French army, which was composed of over half a million soldiers. It was the most dreadful war of liberation in Africa. Independence was gained on July 5, 1962, but at least one million Algerians paid for it with their lives.

The face of English colonialism was revealed in all its brutality in South Africa. The whites possessed 88 percent of the lands, while Black South Africans, by the *Native Lands Act* of 1913, had lost all right of ownership. It was the beginning of the racist policy of segregation of Blacks in "reservations for the Indigenous." But since this procedure did not work, in 1948 the system of apartheid was introduced. In 1949 mixed marriages were prohibited, and in 1950 the population was cataloged under four racial groups: Whites, Indians, People of Color, and Blacks, with the last relegated to territories called *Bantustans*. At least three-quarters of a million Blacks were segregated by force in these zones reserved to them. Meanwhile, Blacks who remained in "white" zones for reasons of work were forbidden access to schools, public places, and means of transport, reserved for whites alone.

The leaders of the anti-apartheid movement, which included Nelson Mandela, were condemned to life imprisonment. But the government's repression did not succeed in suffocating the rebellion of the Africans. Both Black laborers and students gave life to a series of strikes and demonstrations that slowly brought the system of apartheid to a crisis. The turning point occurred in 1990 when Prime Minister Frederik Willem de Klerk announced to Parliament the lifting of the ban against the African National Congress Party and the release of political prisoners. After twenty-seven years of incarceration, Nelson Mandela was liberated. In 1994 the first free elections took place that were not race based, and on May 10, Mandela became the president of South Africa.

Here too, the churches of the whites—Catholic, Anglican, and other Protestant—by a large majority supported the apartheid system. But a small prophetic group—composed of the Catholic archbishop of Durban, Denis Hurley; the pastor of the South African Dutch Reformed Church, Beyers Naudé; and the Anglican Archbishop Desmond Tutu—guided the Black resistance against apartheid.

It was Archbishop Hurley who read apartheid, at base, as a framework of evil:

> It would seem that social behaviors are responsible for the greater part of the evil that rages in the world, great and disastrous evil, which, however, when well analyzed, is not imputable to individuals, or if it is, to very few. . . . One can grow to maturity and beyond in a society that lives and prospers on injustice, such as the White society of South Africa, but without ever being aware of it. One can be part of a great system of evil, without knowing it. And all because of social behaviors. Social behaviors produce institutions, and the institutions, in their turn, perpetuate the behaviors. In this vicious circle the evil institutions are both effect and cause of the social behaviors. Apartheid is one of these evils. . . . The present crisis of South Africa has its origin in the failure of religious and cultural organizations that did not know how to effect a change in the social behaviors of the dominant White minority.

And men of the church, such as Hurley, Tutu, and Naudé, though minorities within their own ecclesiastical world, knew how to instill an enormous hope for liberation.

Belgian colonialism was just as cruel and ruthless. King Leopold II was obsessed with the idea of possessing a colony, and his craving fell upon the basin of the Congo River. To realize his dream he created the International Association of the Congo and financed the English explorer Henry M. Stanley, who, in his voyages along the river and in the name of the association, entered into a series of treaties with the principal locals. Furnished with these treaties, Leopold II attended the Berlin Conference (1884–85), which had been assembled to draw the lines of the European partition of Africa, where he was awarded the Congo Basin. On May 29, the Belgian king proclaimed the "Independent State of the Congo," which became Leopold II's personal property. He divided that enormous territory into blocks entrusted to private companies, to which he granted exclusive right to exploit all natural resources they could remove: ivory, palm oil, copper, tropical woods, but above all rubber, much sought after in Europe.

To force the Africans to harvest rubber (extremely hard labor), the king installed an all-out system of terror. If a village refused obedience (for work that was unpaid!), the company militia would arrive and burn the huts and shoot everyone on sight, killing men, women, and children alike. To make sure that the soldiers really killed villagers, officials required soldiers to cut off the hands of the victims and deliver them to a commissioner, who would then have them counted. A horror, all in the name of profit, all in the name of rubber! It was a carnage that reduced the population of the Congo from about twenty million to eight million by 1911.

During the reign of Leopold II many missionaries, mostly Belgian, went to bring "the gospel" to the Congo, building churches, schools, and dispensaries: "Yet," writes the Ugandan theologian Emmanuel Katongole in his study *The Sacrifice of Africa*, "the role of Christianity remained largely invisible." Western Christianity held that its field of competence was that of the "spiritual" and "pastoral," while politics belonged to the State. According to Katongole, this is the kind of Christianity brought to Africa.

While Leopold II was gobbling up the Congo basin, Germany endeavored to take over territories in Africa, today's Tanzania and Namibia, where the occupation was particularly violent. In 1904, when the Herero and the Nama peoples rebelled against the Germans, Berlin immediately sent an armed contingent commanded by General Lothar von Trotha to repress the revolt. The general's order was peremptory: every Herero found in the lands occupied by the Germans was to be shot. In 1903 about eighty thousand Hereros lived in that territory; in 1906 they were reduced to fifteen thousand, and of these a good nine thousand were held in forced labor camps. Of the twenty thousand Namas, less than half survived. Moreover, the Germans poisoned the wells, another genocide that remains unpunished. The admission that there was any massacre at all came only in 1985, from the UN in the *Whitaker Report*, which defined it as one of the first genocides of the twentieth century. Many scholars consider it to have been a dress rehearsal for the Holocaust. Today the Herero and Nama peoples seek economic reparation, which Berlin has so far denied, for the victims of the genocide; instead, the German government offers a billion euros for "development." "This is a true insult" was the reply of their descendants.

## Italians, Good People![3]

Italy was one of the last European nations to participate in the partitioning of Africa. In 1890 Eritrea became the first Italian colony, and Rome also placed Somalia under its protectorate, making it a colony in 1905. Italy also hoped to seize Ethiopia, ruled by the Emperor Menelik, but it suffered a great defeat, leaving almost five thousand dead on the field. This victory permitted Ethiopia to remain independent and taught the African peoples that the invaders could be beaten. Italy next sought to get its hands on Libya, with an Italian expeditionary force that landed at Tripoli on October 5, 1911. But the invasion of the regions of Tripoli and Cyrene by a military force of more than one hundred thousand unleashed an Arab revolt. This was met with a ferocious repression by the Italians, and thousands of Libyans were hung, shot, or deported. The resistance, however, did not fold, lasting over twenty years, notwithstanding the brutality of the repression, which became even more extreme under the dictatorship of Mussolini.

In 1930, by order of Il Duce,[4] at least one hundred thousand Libyans were deported from Cyrene to isolate the partisans, who were held in concentration camps, in great part afterward shot or hung. The air force was also used, on the order of Mussolini, to exterminate the rebel populations,

---

[3] Translator's note: *Italiani, Brava Gente* (Italians, good people or great people) was the title of a 1964 anti-war movie based on the little-known participation of Italians in the German invasion of Russia in World War II; it has been adopted as a term applying to a historical outlook that minimizes the Italian role in the horrible events of the era.

[4] Translator's note: Il Duce was the Italian nickname for Mussolini; it means "the leader."

using chemical weapons (suffocating gases and mustard-gas bombs). In 1931 the leader of the rebellion, Omar al-Mukhtar (the Lion of the Desert), was located and captured and, after a summary trial, hung before twenty thousand Libyans. It was one of the most ferocious colonial repressions, costing the lives of over one hundred thousand persons.

It was then that Mussolini, after having subdued Libya, decided in 1934 to conquer Ethiopia in the largest colonial expedition, consisting of five hundred thousand men, three hundred fifty airplanes, and two hundred fifty armored vehicles. On October 3, 1935, Italian troops attacked Ethiopia. But more than a colonial war of conquest, it was a war of destruction of the Ethiopian people. Despite fierce resistance, the Italian army had the upper hand, primarily because it used aviation and chemical weapons, even against fleeing troops. The Italian troops used flamethrowers in roundups. There was massacre upon massacre, of helpless populations. On May 5, 1936 Badoglio entered Addis Ababa. That day, from Palazzo Venezia,[5] Mussolini proclaimed to the crowd "the re-establishment of the Empire on the fated hills of Rome. Ethiopia is Italian!" And he imposed on all the colonies the *Race Manifest* of 1938.

All this happened with the blessing of the chief ecclesiastical hierarchy of Italy. Cardinal Schuster of Milan said, in the Cathedral: "We cooperate with God in this national and noble Catholic mission, above all in this moment in which, on the fields of Ethiopia, the Italian flag brings the Cross of

---

[5] Translator's note: Palazzo Venezia in central Rome, near the Colosseum, has a balcony overlooking a huge piazza, or square, of the same name, from which Mussolini delivered speeches to masses of Italians assembled there.

Christ in triumph, breaks the chains, and levels the roads for the missionaries of the Gospel." And further: "God will give peace and protection to the valorous army which in fearless obedience, at the command of the fatherland, at the cost of blood, opens the gates of Ethiopia to the Catholic faith and to Roman civilization." Many other Italian bishops said the same.

In Italy, unfortunately, the political decision was made to hide the true nature of the harm and to promote the idea that Italian colonialism would be benevolent. Nevertheless, historians like Angelo del Boca and Georgio Rochat wrote volumes about the ferocity of Italian colonialism.

When will not only the Italian people, but the entire white world, have the courage to admit the crimes committed in the colonial era in Africa? When, in the end, will we in Italy recognize our own shameful colonial history?

## The Theory of Race

In the nineteenth century the colonial occupation of the Black continent was prepared and justified by a series of pseudo-scientific theories focusing on the superiority of the White race over the Black.

European anthropology of the nineteenth century undertook the classification, claiming a scientific basis, of the populations of the various continents according to the color of their skin and various other physical characteristics, to define their "race." This brought about the classification of nine human races. Clearly, in its own eyes, the white race held first place, a position that it perceived gave it the natural right to colonize the various continents, to bring "civilization."

"The study of psychology in Eastern Africa is the study of man's rudimental mind," wrote the English explorer Richard Burton from Lake Tanganyika in his 1860 *The Lake Regions of Central Africa*. "He would appear rather a degeneracy from the civilized man than a savage rising to the first step, were it not for his apparent incapacity for improvement."

This racial prejudice took on a "scientific" character, above all, in France and England. Pioneering the effort was Scottish doctor Robert Knox, who had founded a school of anatomy. He held that the "dark races" were necessarily destined to *extinction*. This theory was soon absorbed by the European elites, including Italians, and became the central element of the imperialist ideology. "Abyssinia[6] must be ours," affirmed General Antonio Baldissera in 1891, "because such is the lot of the inferior races: the Blacks little by little are disappearing and we must bring civilization to Africa, not for the Abyssinians, but for ourselves."

In Germany anthropologist Friedrich Ratzel made this theory his own and integrated it with the theory of "room to live."[7] Given that the space on earth is limited, the superior races, he asserted, had the right to replace the races of inferior culture. Among the "lesser" Ratzel included the Africans, gypsies, and Jews. This also formed the ideological basis of Nazism and fascism. The result was the Holocaust:

---

[6] Translator's note: Abyssinia was a name for Ethiopia before the conquest by Italy in 1936.

[7] Translator's note: The German word *Lebensraum,* derived from the words for "life" or "living" and for "room" or "space," was later adopted by the Nazis as justification of their policies of conquest of Germany's neighbors that initiated World War II in Europe; it is here rendered as "room to live."

six million Jews and half a million Roma ended up in crematory ovens.

Enslavement and colonialism gave birth to the great wealth and the riches of the West. But they also marked that wealth with the claim of white racial superiority that led to it. From this was born the "racial supremacy" that, like a cancer, continues to corrupt our Western society. And it is only by beginning with this history of ours that we can understand the growing racism in our midst today. We Italians thought we have no racists. But now we must finally admit that we do. It is enough to read the insults that circulate on social media against the Roma, the migrants, the Jews.

White supremacy, which today is appearing in strength in Europe, in the USA, in Brazil, in Australia, has its roots in this sordid history of slavery and colonialism. It is the bitter fruit from the White Tribe and its mission to "civilize" the world, convinced the white world possessed *civilization, culture,* and *religion*. It is unbelievable how many churches today provide ideological support to white supremacy.

✧ ✧ ✧

Now I would like to share my own personal reflections on racism within human society. I am well aware that racism, as the rejection of the "other," is not a characteristic only of the White Tribe, but of all the tribes of earth, of every human being. I learned that precise lesson in my twelve years with "the least" of this world, the people of the shantytown of Korogocho.

When I descended into the "underworld" there, I was convinced that among the poorest there would be greater capacity to welcome, to accept. But to my great surprise I discovered that anyone who is a little better off among the shantytown people doesn't want anything to do with those they consider the "throwaways": the garbage pickers in the dump, the street children, the girls who turn to prostitution to survive. And I saw this phenomenon even in the small Christian community of Korogocho, which put up the same resistance as those in the White Tribe to accepting those who were "different." I recall the resistance I met with when seeking the participation in the Sunday Eucharist of the garbage pickers of the dump.

"Racism exists everywhere people live," writes Tahar Ben Jelloun in the profound book *Racism Explained to My Daughter*:

> No country can claim to be free of racism. Racism is part of human history. It's better to know about it and learn to fight it. You have to watch yourself and think: "If I'm afraid of foreigners, they must be afraid of me." We're always a foreigner to someone. Learning to live together is how we fight racism.

So it is clear that racism, the fear and the rejection of the "other," is not peculiar to the White Tribe, but a phenomenon common to all peoples, to all societies. Yet the racism of the superiority of the White Tribe is a phenomenon more grave than that of the others, rooted as it is in centuries of dominance over the peoples of the world, with the pretext of the superiority of its own civilization, culture, and religion. This is why we must not forget the history of the White Tribe.

"Some would have us believe that we cannot criticize, in any way, the history of colonial greed and its blindness," asserts the writer Lilian Thuram,[8] a native of Guadeloupe, in his great treatise *White Thinking*, in which he declares: "People aren't born White, they become White. . . . They invite us to forget. And yet it is precisely this forgetting that stops us from 'moving on.'" He concludes: "As far as I'm concerned, the only duty of any value for White people acting in good faith is to try to understand what has happened over the centuries, and to note what remains of it in today's behaviors."

That is, to observe what have been the mechanisms of white dominance, what have been the most recurrent justifications, and how they reverberate the past in the present.

And what are today's "good reasons" used to justify the inferiorization of non-whites, the savage exploitation of a part of the world, and the looting of its natural resources?

---

[8] Translator's note: To a great many of Zanotelli's Italian readers, as devotees of European football (American soccer), a sport which dominates all others in Italy as practically the national pastime, Lilian Thuram would be well known. Black, and born in the West Indies on the island of Guadeloupe, a territory that has full status as a Department of France, he attained a prestigious international career in European football with the French national team as World Champions in 1998 and European Champions in 2006, as well as with the prestigious European teams, Juventus in Italy, and Barcelona in Spain. In 2008 he created the Lilian Thuram Foundation for Education against Racism. In 2020 he wrote *White Thinking*, quoted here, which might be described as a meditation on relations between races, based on his reflections on and analysis of centuries of history, which he described as an effort to contribute to "dialogue" in the hope of helping to provide "tools to construct a shared future."

# 4

# White Supremacy

### Injustice Built into the System

Multi-century dominion has made the White Tribe a world power. Europe, the United States, Canada, and Australia today constitute the heart of the world economy and finance. About 10 percent of the world population (in good part made up of the White Tribe) alone consumes about 90 percent of the goods produced, leaving the crumbs to the rest.

Two billion persons suffer from food insecurity (to which 250 million post-COVID poor must be added), 690 million of whom suffer severely. While the rich 10 percent annually throw away *2,600 billion tons* of good food, every ten seconds a child dies of hunger. Two thousand super rich hold greater wealth than that owned by 4.5 billion people, while 3.8 billion people must be content with 1 percent of the wealth. One person in three does not have access to drinkable water, and 4.2 billion do not have access to health and sanitation services.

Ten percent of the world, to defend its wealth, spent 1,981 billion dollars in 2020 on arms. In 2019 the NATO countries (USA, Europe, Canada), plus Australia, spent 1,035 billion dollars on arms. The United States alone spent 1,000 billion dollars by the time of the Obama presidency in order to update its atomic weapons.

Few have grasped the reason for all these atomic weapons so well as the then-Archbishop of Seattle, Raymond Hunthausen, who in a "Faith and Disarmament" speech given on June 12, 1981, said:

> Propaganda and a particular way of life have clothed us to death.... Nuclear arms protect privilege and exploitation. Giving them up would mean our having to give up economic power over other peoples.... Peace and justice go together. On the path we now follow, our economic policies toward other countries require nuclear weapons. Giving up the weapons would mean giving up more than our means of global terror. It would mean giving up the reason for the terror—our privileged place in the world.

But this economic-financial-military system weighs so heavily on the planet as to put the entire economic system at risk. This is due to the life style of 10 percent of the world population, and due to armaments, to wars, and to the use of fossil fuels for energy. These are the reasons why the richest 10 percent of humanity, using coal and oil, releases billions of tons of carbon dioxide into the atmosphere, which trap some of the sun's heat, and cause global warming. And it is the impoverished who suffer the consequences.

Today it is Africa's turn, the poorest continent, to pay the costs: growing desertification in the Sahel zone[1] and

---

[1] Translator's note: The semi-arid transition region between the Sahara desert and the savanna to the south.

devastating rains in the sub-Saharan zone. One of the grave consequences of this economic-financial-militarized system suffocating the planet is the phenomenon of migration, a bitter fruit of a wicked system.

It is this system that, by impoverishing the majority of the world population, forces millions of people to abandon their lands in search of hope. It is this system that, by causing dreadful wars, such as those in Afghanistan, Iraq, Libya, and Congo over possession of oil and other valuable resources, forces millions of people to flee to save their lives.

It is this system that, by suffocating the earth, causes millions of climatic migrants to flee. There are 250 million migrants in the world. But as I wrote earlier, the UN recognizes as refugees—that is, those with the right of international asylum—only people who flee from war or persecution. This excludes economic migrants and climate migrants. According to the World Bank, environmental migrations will displace 143 million people by 2050. Other estimates are as high as 200 million.

Today the UN recognizes 82 million people as refugees, in flight from wars and persecution. And these refugees are knocking at the doors of the rich world. Those of the Asiatic subcontinent seek to reach Australia. Refugees from Africa and the Middle East knock on the doors of Europe, while those of Latin America press toward the United States.

It is incredible, though, that 86 percent of refugees do not arrive at the rich world but at the impoverished countries: Uganda receives over a million from South Sudan; Kenya gives welcome to several million from Somalia; Lebanon to over a million Syrians. In contrast, the rich world does not want to receive the impoverished of the world.

Under Trump, the United States barred the doors to persons from Central and South America, seeking to build a border wall, what some have referred to as a wall of shame. Under Biden those policies of refusing migrants continued. Australia, an immense continent, has enacted draconian legislation to block the impoverished of Southeast Asia, while the refugees from Africa, the Middle East, and Central Asia press against the borders of the European Union. But Europe, too, the third economic power of the world, wants nothing to do with receiving anyone who knocks on its door. And it accomplishes this by "externalizing its border."

The European Union, in fact, uses Turkey, Greece, Italy, and Spain to do its dirty work, to keep migrants as far as possible from Europe (with the exception of isolated Greek and Spanish islands and two Spanish African "possessions," Ceuta and Melilla). The EU has signed an accord with Turkey's Erdogan, giving him six billion euros to restrain, on Turkish territory, at least four million Afghan, Syrian, and Iraqi refugees. And with the renewal of the accord, another 3.5 billion euros was scheduled to be disbursed to Turkey. All of these are defined by the UN as "refugees," with the right of international asylum, because they are fleeing from dreadful wars set off by the West in its own interests.

The European Union entered into another accord, with Greece, to hold back, on its islands, thousands of refugees forced to vegetate in the mud of their camps. Lesbos is a squalid example of this, where some 7,300 migrants are held in the Kara Tepe camp, of whom 2,500 are children; forty-nine of them have attempted suicide. The European Union has also reached an agreement with Spain to hold intercepted migrants in Morocco at Ceuta and Melilla and to hold those seeking to reach Europe by sea in the Canary Islands.

And, lastly, there is the basic agreement that the European Union has made with Italy, using it to externalize the European border at Libya and Tunisia. In fact, by means of a Memorandum of Understanding with the government of Tripoli, Italy holds in the Libyan concentration camps up to half a million refugees, where they are treated as beasts. And this is done with our money and that of the European Union.

In addition, Italy finances the Libyan Coast Guard in going to sea to re-apprehend those who attempt to flee. In 2021 as many as 31,456 refugees were intercepted and brought back to the Libyan concentration camps.

Italy does the dirty work for Brussels, which pursues an unacceptable migration policy. "To say that in a continent with 500 million inhabitants it is not possible to accept 5 million people is a total absurdity," rightly asserts the noted Swiss activist Jean Ziegler in *Lesbos, the Shame of Europe*. "We live in a world system that on one hand guarantees security and well being to one part of the world's population, and on the other lets a child die of [preventable causes] every five seconds, while the current agricultural resources could feed 12 billion people."

Not only does Europe externalize the border, but it also erects barbed-wire barriers within its own interior. Spain began with the barriers at Ceuta and Melilla in Morocco, followed by Hungary, which has constructed a wall of steel almost 110 miles long, at the cost of 21 million euros. Greece, too, has built a barrier of steel, sixteen feet high, on its border with Turkey, while Poland is erecting a wall along the border with Belarus. So also Bulgaria, with a 145-mile barrier preventing arrivals from Turkey. The list continues: anti-migrant walls have been raised by Slovenia and Austria as well. Moreover, twelve states of the European Union have sent a letter to the European Commission to ask it to finance new anti-immigrant barriers. A 2019 survey by YouGov shows that, regrettably, over half of all Europeans are in favor of such walls.

Here we have truly arrived at the absurd. After centuries of enslavement and colonialism that allowed the West to plunder the peoples of the world and enrich itself on their backs, now the White Tribe closes itself off and armors itself to keep out those we have impoverished who now stand knocking at our door. This is perhaps the ultimate hubris, egoism, in human history.

Professor Luigi Ferrajoli, a philosopher of jurisprudence, in the November 20, 2020, edition of the periodical *il manifesto*, articulates how this constitutes a blatant contradiction for the European Union:

> The European Union was born to put an end to racism, to discrimination and to genocides: not to divide and exclude, but to unite and include on the basis of basic rights shared by all. Now it is upending that role. It is, with laws against immigration (today's race laws), increasing inequalities of status, by birth, between *citizens with full rights; second class citizens* with more or less stable legalization; and *illegal immigrants*, reduced to the status of persons who are "illegal," or non-persons. Above all, it is unleashing, by a huge dearth of aid, a new *genocide*, though one by omission: that is, of the migrants who flee from wars, from terror, and from their

cities reduced to piles of rubble, who every year drown in the sea, by the thousands, in the attempt to reach Europe and who, by the hundreds of thousands, crowd at our borders against barriers and barbed wire, left in the cold, hungry, dispersed and ill-treated by our police.

And much is happening in a brutal manner on the border between Belarus and Poland. The consequences of all this are devastating. "The inhuman treatment inflicted on this mass of refugees," concludes Ferrajoli, "in flight from wars and devastation unleashed in great part by our insane policies, has, as its effect, the *growth of hatred toward the West*, and therefore, the enlargement of the *breeding ground of terror*."

## A Disgraceful History

It is only by looking this disgraceful and tragic history in the face that we can try to understand the phenomenon of white supremacy being born in the United States, above all in the South, often called the Bible Belt. Let us not forget that the southern states flourished thanks to the enslavement of millions of Africans who were reduced to chattel (property). The American War of Independence against England (1776) brought no freedom to Black Americans. The beautiful American Declaration of Independence, based on the rights of man, was written by Thomas Jefferson, himself an owner of slaves, who certainly did not intend these "rights of man" to extend to those who were enslaved! The rights he envisioned were only for whites. This original sin has and will continue to grievously stain the history of the United States.

The enslaved in the southern states represented the basis of the wealth of the whites, due to their hard labor on the plantations. "The work of the slaves permitted the English colonies of the South to produce vast quantities of cotton, of rice, and of tobacco that were transported to England and then sold in Europe," writes Manlio Dinucci in his well-wrought book *Geostoria dell'Africa* (the geohistory of Africa). At the same time, the English colonies of the northeast also benefited from the slave trade, whether by furnishing foodstuffs or by providing shipping services for the transport of the goods produced to Europe.

This economic structure based on slavery continued after the war of liberation and the independence of the colonies from England (1776). This economic superiority allowed the northern states to prevail when conflicts of interest caused the outbreak of the Civil War (1861–65), with their victory in that dreadful war. It was President Abraham Lincoln, toward the end of the war, who proclaimed the emancipation of the slaves.

"Lincoln . . . combined perfectly the needs of business, the political ambition of the new Republican Party, and the rhetoric of humanitarianism," writes Howard Zinn in his extraordinary book *A People's History of the United States*. "He would keep the abolition of slavery not at the top of his list of priorities, but close enough to the top so it could be pushed there temporarily by abolitionist pressures and by practical political advantage." Unfortunately this decision was not of great benefit to the enslaved, who found themselves with nothing in their hands within the deeply racist structures in the South, as well as in the North, where many migrated in search of work in the great cities. And so racism, though in a different form and expression, became a structural component within the American system. Continuing even now.

"The lynching of black America," asserts James Cone in his book *The Cross and the Lynching Tree*,

> is taking place in the criminal justice system where nearly one-third of black men between the ages of eighteen and twenty-eight are in prisons, jails, on parole, or waiting for their day in court. Nearly one-half of the more than two million people in prisons are black. That is one million black people behind bars, more than in colleges. Through private prisons and the "war against drugs," whites have turned the brutality of their racist legal system into a profit-making venture for dying white towns and cities throughout America. Michelle Alexander correctly calls America's criminal justice system "the new Jim Crow." "The criminalization and demonization of black men," writes Alexander, "is one habit that America seems unlikely to break without addressing head-on the racial dynamics that have given rise to our latest caste system." Nothing is more racist in America's criminal justice system than its administration of the death penalty. America is the only industrialized country in the West where the death penalty is still legal. Most countries regard it as both immoral and barbaric. But not in America. The death penalty is primarily reserved, though not exclusively, for people of color, and white supremacy shows no signs of changing it. That is why the term *legal lynching* is still relevant today. One can lynch a person without a rope or tree.

Another Black theologian, Dominique Du Bois Gilliard, is profoundly right when, in *Rethinking Incarceration,* he writes: "Racism is part of the anatomy of the United States: we have always been a racist nation. Whiteness is associated with citizenship, with integrity, with 'law and order,' while dark pigment is connected to the suspect, to criminality, and to the deviant."

## The Complicity of the Churches

Unfortunately, many of the churches in the United States even today are an integral part of this white supremacy. "The church cannot aspire to neutrality," writes American theologian Katie Grimes in her 2015 piece "Telling Tales: Ferguson and the Church" on the Women in Theology website. "Rather than mediating between two sides, the church ought to take the side of those who struggle against white supremacy most boldly. But the church cannot do this until it learns to prefer the racial chaos that looks like violence to the white supremacist violence that passes for peace." But it will not be easy for the churches of the whites to accomplish this change of direction, given their complicity with the racist structures and their attachment to white supremacy.

The evangelical churches of the South were deeply complicit with white supremacy. With the rise of the Ku Klux Klan, one of the most notorious racist organizations of the South, many White Christians behaved as if lynching Blacks were a legitimate defense of their very civilization. Frank Morris, a pastor of a large fundamentalist church in Fort Worth, had the effrontery to invite the Grand Dragon of the Klan to lead the Sunday prayer in his church. In the 1950s and

1960s, the powerful union of the Baptist Churches of the South opposed the civil rights movement of the Blacks. In 1956 Pastor Wallie Amos Criswell of the First Baptist Church of Dallas dared to denounce publicly the decision of the Supreme Court that had declared racial segregation unconstitutional.

To reconcile racial apartheid with the Christian faith, white segregationists developed a theological system of defense. If the scope of Christianity is that of saving souls to bring them to paradise, then preoccupation with injustice in this world lay outside the scope of the gospel. If personal sin was what counted, then the important thing for white Christians was to live justly, even within a system of racial apartheid. For them, racism was a personal sin, not anything structural.

In a 1964 article titled "Race as a Principality in the Church," William Stringfellow, one of the most penetrating Christian thinkers in the United States, wrote: "To no principality . . . have the American churches been more notoriously and scandalously and complacently accommodating than to the principality of racism." Baptist pastor Eugene F. Rivers III, who met Stringfellow in 1973, wrote in "The Idol of White Supremacy" (*Sojourners*, March-April 1997):

> I want to expand this notion to include . . . white supremacy, as the dominant principality of America. White identity splits the country in two and is now poised to generate civil war in the United States. . . .
>
> We've spent 300 years developing this idolatry, and it is now deeply entrenched in the cultural psychology of the nation and the church. Only a radical conversion to biblical faith frees us from the burden of this demonic

spirit that binds us and renders us unable to live as rational human beings.

He calls white identity an "ideological concept" that was "demonically inspired." He asserts that "white racism, the concrete expression of . . . white supremacy, is demonically entrenched," and calls upon "church people, especially white church people . . . to choose between being the church and being white." After digging deeper, he concludes with a weighty question:

> White racist ideology is . . . based on pride. . . . Pride is an ideology and a concept of identity that is against God in its essence. It is atheistic. It is demonic. And so the challenge now is, "Will we be white or will we be the church?"

## The Epiphany[2] of the White Supremacists

This choice—to be white or to be a church—became clear on January 6, 2021, when a white mob provoked by then-president of the United States, Donald Trump, invaded Capitol Hill, precisely at the moment when the members of the Senate and House of Representatives were to certify the results of the election of Joe Biden. It was truly an attempted coup that left everyone stunned. Among the crowd was the entire galaxy of white supremacist actors. Conspicuous was the Shaman of QAnon, a group of conspiracy theorists who

---

[2] Translator's note: In the Catholic Church the feast of the Epiphany is celebrated yearly on January 6 and represents the public revelation of the newborn child Christ to the world (symbolized in the person of the three kings, or magi). The parallel is to the "revelation" of white supremacists who took part in the events on that date in Washington, DC.

hold that an occult power colluded with a network of pedophiles and prominent Democrats, in particular Hillary Clinton and Barack Obama. There were the Proud Boys (called "patriots" by Trump), a violent group of white supremacists with a neo-fascist stamp. The Proud Boys, founded in 2017 by radio commentator Gavin McInnes to defend Western values, did not accept women among their ranks and were convinced that COVID-19 was just an excuse for gun control and seizure. And then there were the Boogaloo, who were armed to the teeth, wearing military uniforms. They made their first public appearance during the lockdown of April 2020. Also present were the Oath Keepers, founded by Stewart Rhodes, many of whom later faced charges of seditious conspiracy.[3] The other important ultra-right presence consisted of those who were part of the alt-right, made up of disparate and unorganized groups. Their manifesto held three main points. First, men are under attack, and no to feminism. Second, language is under attack, because use of racist and sexist language is being denounced. Third, the white race is under attack, and waves of migrants crossing the border threaten the purity of the white race. Starting from the assumption that races exist as a matter of biology, the alt-right found in Donald Trump, with his anti-migrant and racist policies, the perfect candidate for the presidency of the United States.

It is unbelievable that a crowd succeeded in breaking through and occupying Capitol Hill despite barriers, police, and security measures. Today, thanks to the investigation by the House of Representatives, we know that the assault on

---

[3] Translator's note: Rhodes was convicted in November of 2022 and sentenced in 2023 to eighteen years imprisonment for seditious conspiracy.

the Congress was not a simple pro-Trump demonstration but was the fruit of planning begun months beforehand by a group of the tycoon's lawyers, including Rudy Giuliani, and his chief of staff Mark Meadows, as well as a number of Republican House members. The "brains" behind the plan seems to have been the well-known Steve Bannon, mastermind behind the idea of January 6. According to the Select Committee of the House, Bannon "urged then-President Trump to pressure then-Vice President Michael R. Pence to assist in overturning the results of the 2020 election, by refusing to certify the electoral votes of certain states." It was truly an attempted coup.

Unfortunately, we will not easily free ourselves from Trumpism and from his supporters, the white supremacists. Trump still has a strong hold on the Republicans, running again in 2024. In February 2021, at a Conference in Orlando for a conservative PAC (political action committee), 95 percent of the Republicans present expressed the desire to continue the policies of the Trump administration and defend white supremacy. By the summer of 2024, Trump was already revving up his engines to become the new president of the United States in 2025.

## The Genocide of the "Indians"

To understand white supremacy we must also analyze another fundamental historical phenomenon: the elimination of Indigenous peoples, the so-called Indians, the first inhabitants of North America. All native peoples on the continent had distinctive names: the Arawak, the Cherokee, the Sioux. But white people, believing themselves to have arrived in what are now called the East Indies, called them all Indians.

Just reading *A People's History of the United States* by the previously noted historian Howard Zinn is enough to shift one's awareness and aid in beginning to understand colonial powers—the English colonists in North America were following the plan of action adopted by Columbus in the Bahamas: massacre and enslave Indigenous peoples. "Columbus and his successors were not coming into an empty wilderness," asserts Zinn,

> but into a world which in some places was as densely populated as Europe itself, where the culture was complex, where human relations were more egalitarian than in Europe, and where the relations among men, women, children, and nature were more beautifully worked out than perhaps any place in the world.

In North America, Indigenous peoples were confronted by the brute force of the English colonists. In 1585 Richard Grenville landed in Virginia with seven ships and found the Indians hospitable, until one of them stole a small silver cup. In response, Grenville razed the entire village to the ground. From that beginning arose war with various native nations. When the Pellegrini Fathers arrived in New England, that land was inhabited by Indigenous people, but the governor of the Massachusetts Bay Colony labeled it "No Man's Land"; the "Indians" had only "natural" right, not "civil" right, to the land, thus stoking the war against the "Indians" there, which would end only in 1676, with their defeat.

Later, to free the territories from the Appalachian mountains to the Mississippi, so they could be settled by the whites, the colonists resorted to the "transfer of the Indians" (the *Indian Removal Act*), as it was euphemistically called.

This made an immense territory available for the cultivation of cotton in the South and of grains in the North, for immigration and for expansion, an expansion which would eventually arrive at the Pacific Ocean. And the Indigenous peoples were either massacred, or confined in reservations, as if to be viewed by tourists. Many died, also, from diseases brought with them by the Whites.

The ten million Indigenous people who lived north of Mexico at the time of Columbus's arrival were reduced, eventually, to less than one million. It was another genocide perpetrated by the White Tribe. "The landing of Christopher Columbus in the New World initiated a genocide," asserts Zinn, "which involved the violent expulsion of Indians, accompanied by unspeakable atrocities, from every square mile of the continent, until there was nothing left to do with them but herd them into reservations."

The harms of the white world continue. Leonard Peltier, an iconic figure of native peoples in North America, is one of the historical leaders of the American Indian Movement (AIM). Since 1977, for almost fifty years, he has been rotting in inhuman conditions in a maximum security prison. A persecuted political figure, he has been condemned as a result of a trial marked by multiple violations of his rights during his defense. World famous personages have requested, and are still requesting, his release.

All that happened not just in places now within the United States, but also nearby in Canada, also occupied by English colonists. In Canada a true cultural genocide was unleashed against the Indigenous populations, a genocide too long denied.

"Kill the Indian, save the man" went the racist motto adopted by the Canadian schools in which Indigenous children suffered the cancellation of their culture. On May 29, 2021, near the school of Kamloops, the remains of 215 native children were discovered. A few days later came another horrible discovery: the bodies of 750 children buried near a Catholic church in Saskatchewan, Canada. Many researchers suspect that there were secret burials of many thousands of children to hide the shame of the genocide.

These macabre discoveries open an ugly page of Canada's past. Between 1863 and 1998, 150,000 native children were torn from their families by the Canadian government and relocated in residential schools to force them to accept Western religion and civilization. Among the 118 residential schools, 79 were Catholic and were directly subject to the Vatican. In these schools there were many instances of violence, sterilizations, and rapes.

How was it possible for all this to happen? To understand it, one must go back to Canadian legislation. The *Federal Indian Act* of 1874, still in force, proclaims the legal and moral inferiority of Indigenous peoples. Another federal decree, the *Gradual Civilization Act* (1857), obliged the families of native peoples to sign a document that transferred the right of guardianship of the children to residential schools. We must not forget that the legal transfer of the right of guardianship of minors meant that, in the event of death, the schools benefited, taking ownership of their land.

Finally, in British Columbia, another decree, the *Sterilization Law* of 1933 (still on the books), permitted the mass sterilization of entire groups of Indigenous children. Amnesty International has denounced the fact that many Indigenous women, who had gone to the hospital for childbirth, came home sterilized.

We are looking at a real cultural genocide, one which brought about the elimination of Indigenous languages as well as the suppression of native culture and spirituality, with complete political and economic marginalization.

They became foreigners in their own lands.

## Latin America

It is not only in the United States that white supremacy is winning out. We are finding it ever strengthening in Latin America, in Australia, and in Europe.

In Latin America the White Tribe took over by conquest, with the slaughter of Indigenous peoples and the imposition of "Christian civilization." In the last thirty years the fundamentalist Christian groups and the evangelical churches coming from the United States have found fertile ground there. Today white supremacy is penetrating into almost all the countries of Latin America.

Perhaps the most striking case is its triumph in Brazil. "We are in a country," affirms the Brazilian philosopher Djamila Ribeiro in *Where We Stand,*

> which has long denied the existence of racism. Brazil was one of the last to abolish slavery (1888), which was at the base of the Brazilian economy. The liberated slaves had neither land, nor rights. Instead, the government favored European immigration, for the "whitening" of the

Brazilian population, and, to these, it gave land. Brazil did not have legal segregation as in the United States, but it had, and still has, a type of institutional segregation. The poor population is poor because it is Black.

It is within this milieu that the evangelical churches of the United States have succeeded in penetrating into the fabric of Brazil and in becoming so strong as to torpedo the government of Dilma Rousseff, and then support the election of former military Jair Bolsonaro, who is carrying out homophobic, sexist, and xenophobic policies. Bolsonaro has sold Brazil to the multinationals who are destroying Amazonia. And, as a good follower of the fundamentalist and denialist churches, he did nothing to impede the COVID-19 pandemic, bringing Brazil into a health crisis.

In neighboring Colombia, the peace accords between the government and FARC (Fuerzas Armadas Revolucionarias de Columbia, the Revolutionary Armed Forces of Columbia) have failed because evangelical and Catholic fundamentalists there oppose the accords, maintaining they support abortion rights and homosexuality. Then, in Bolivia, the military and fundamentalist religious groups successfully supported a coup against Evo Morales, the president of the republic, who was guilty only of having given priority of place, policy, culture, and economy to Indigenous peoples, who had always suffered the crush of colonial power. And they orchestrated that coup with the Bible and the crucifix in hand. But in the elections of October 18, 2020, the citizenry gave an absolute majority (53 percent) to the Movement for Socialism (MAS), electing Luis Arce, an ex-minister under Morales, as president of the republic.

The same is happening in Central America. In Costa Rica evangelical pastor Fabricio Alvarado won the presidential elections in 2018 with a platform in favor of "Christian values," opposing abortion, and supporting other policies now often called neoliberalism. In El Salvador, the president of the republic, Nayib Bukele, at his installation ceremony invited the Argentinian evangelical pastor Dante Gebel, with close ties to ultraconservative pastors in the United States, to offer the prayer. And a deputy presented a motion in parliament to impose the obligatory reading of the Bible in all schools.

These are just some examples of a movement that we might call international Christo-neo-fascist, neoliberal, and patriarchal. In Latin America it is the reaction of the White Tribe in defense of its supremacy, using the "gospel of prosperity" to legitimize its predominating neoliberalism.

## Australia

This is also evident in Australia, which is now the domain of the White Tribe. Upon the first voyage of James Cook, in 1770, the Australian continent was declared No Man's Land, with Aboriginal peoples considered little more than animals. They were not counted in the census; they could not possess land.

In 1994 the Australian Parliament received the *Stolen Generation* report that documented how for decades White Australia had taken children from their Aboriginal families to raise them in white families or in religious institutions, for forced integration. The enforced policy involved tearing children away from their parents, from their land, and from their memories, to inculcate new "Christian" principles into their minds.

From their beginnings in 1869, the forced removals continued until 1969, with some places continuing into the 1970s. It is now acknowledged by all that this mass removal was rooted in a fear of racial mixing among Aboriginal people and white Europeans—or even in the desire to reach a "white purity" on the part of the dominant white classes. It was truly a cultural genocide, like that effectuated by the White Tribe of Canada. Only in 1967 did a referendum declare Aboriginal peoples Australian citizens.

To maintain its "whiteness," Australia has favored European immigration. Today it is a continent of the White Tribe that relegates Aboriginal people to the most marginalized zones even as it refuses migrants coming from Asia as Australia tightens its policy, removing the "boat people."

"No one requesting asylum, arriving by boat to settle in Australia, will ever be authorized to settle on our territory as a refugee," said the then Prime Minister Kevin Rudd. This policy, launched at the beginning of the century, rests on accords with two remote islands of Oceania. To effectuate this, Australia made agreements with two nearby states, the Republic of Nauru and the islet of Manus (Papua New Guinea), two centers for permanent detention of refugees, with the only alternative for those detained being repatriation. Since 2012 more than four thousand men, women, and children have been transported to those concentration camps, where many have suffered mental illness. In 2018 the center at Manus was closed and those detained were abandoned at Port-Moresby, the capital of Papua New Guinea. That was the "externalization of the borders," inspiring European governments to follow in kind.

## Europe, the Homeland of the White Tribe

The pandemic of white supremacy is spreading like a weed in Europe, too. Let us not forget that Europe was a fertile ground for both Nazism, with the physical elimination of millions of Jews, Roma, and homosexuals; and for fascism, with the *Race Manifest* and the racial laws of Mussolini.

Today the "extreme right of God," as Spanish theologian Juan Tamayo calls it, is expanding in Europe, from Spain to the Urals.

In Spain there is a remarkable concordance between Spanish Catholic organizations and the ultra-conservative HartetOir, El Yunque, InfoCatolica, and others like the extreme right party Vox, which is steadily gaining support, as well as political importance. Even the leader of the Brothers of Italy, Giorgia Meloni, participated at the Vox convention in 2021.[4] Vox in reality wants to build its own wall around Ceuta and Melilla[5] to stop migrants. And also in Portugal the extreme right populist party Chega is steadily gaining support.

In France it is the National Rally party (until 2018 it was called National Front) that is the voice of the extreme right. Founded by Jean-Marie Le Pen, the National Front supported a French identity that was against integration, denied the Holocaust, and maintained ties to neo-fascist groups. In the last European elections the National Rally, led by Marine Le Pen, daughter of party founder Jean-Marie, received five million votes. And for the elections of 2022, in France there was the new ultra-right phenomenon of Eric Zemmour: misogynistic, homophobic, Islamophobic, and racist.

---

[4] Translator's note: Giorgia Meloni, as of 2023, as the leader of the Brothers of Italy party, became the prime minister of Italy.

[5] Translator's note: As peviously mentioned, Ceuta and Melilla are small Spanish "possessions" in North Africa.

He maintains that the party of Marine Le Pen is neither harsh nor racist enough. "The obsession of Zemmour is Islam." His theory is that of replacement of one racial group by another, "because," he asserts, "there is a colonization in progress, by foreigners." On November 30, 2021, he officially entered the French presidential race, and on December 5, to support his candidacy, he founded the political party Reconquete (Reconquest), a clear historical reference to the Spanish "Reconquista" that fought against Muslim rule. He has the support of bankers, reactionary millionaires, the media of Bollore, as well as a portion of the Catholic world.

In Austria it was Jorg Haider who in 1993 launched with his FPO party (Party of Austrian Liberty) the Austria First campaign, with the goal of introducing more severe laws against immigration. In the elections of 1999 Haider obtained historic numbers, carrying his party to become the second party of the country, though he then lost support due to the scandal that also involved the leader of the FPO, Heinz C. Strache. The various succeeding governments of Austria have thereafter maintained policies of a strong populist, identity, and anti-immigration thrust.

In nearby Germany the racist party Alternative for Germany (AFD) is steadily gaining ground and has had growth in eastern Germany and in Saxony, while gaining support in Bavaria, too. In fact, in the quite wealthy and Catholic Bavaria, which struggles to find a labor force for about thirty thousand positions, there is yet a growing rejection of the Syrian migrants permitted entry by Angela Merkel. The middle class fears the loss of its status and wealth, and it is pushing to preserve them by building border walls. There are over twelve thousand members of neo-Nazi groups in Germany. And a confidential report of Europol asserts that these groups are showing a growing interest in taking up arms.

To the east and southeast of Germany there are three nations that are creating a fear in Europe related to their extreme right positions: Hungary, Romania, and Poland. Hungary is led by Viktor Orban, whose party Fidesz reached 52.3 percent of the vote. Orban shuttered all critical daily newspapers and is mobilizing the country against migrants. He has sealed the Hungarian border with barbed wire to prevent the entrance of migrants into the country, a wall of steel almost 110 miles long, at a cost of 21 million euros.

In Romania, with the elections of December 6, 2020, another party gained entry into Parliament that is still further to the right than Orban in Hungary: the Alliance for the Union of Romanians (AUR). Its supporters have shared conspiracy theories about COVID-19 and refused to wear masks. They are even more pronounced in their hostility to foreigners. In Romania, too, both the Protestant hierarchy and that of the Catholics share the ideas of Orban.

The same climate is in the nearby Poland of Jaroslaw Kaczynski, who is leader of the Law and Justice party (PIS), which obtained 45.4 percent of the vote in the last elections. It is an anti-Europe and anti-migrant party and defends "family values" and a conservative church. The murder of the mayor of Danzig, Pawel Adamowicz, is a sign that the struggle in Poland has reached a critical threshold. His violent death dramatically shows the contrast between the reactionary governing party, inspired by Kaczynski, and the liberal opposition, symbolized by the mayor of Danzig, who was known for his openness to migrants, and to the EU and its policies, in contrast to the many far-right nationalists in many countries of Europe, who oppose them.

Unfortunately, the Catholic Church in Poland is supportive of the government and shares its choices. In fact, on October 7, 2017, the episcopal conference of Poland invited Catholics to place themselves along the 2,200 miles of its borders, with rosary in hand, "to safeguard Poland and Europe from Islamic nihilism and the disavowal of the Christian faith."

Every year the Catholic Church celebrates the feast of Our Lady of the Rosary on that date, October 7. But that date is also meaningful because it's a nod to the anniversary of the Battle of Lepanto, which in 1571 stopped the advance of the Turks into Europe. This effort to "safeguard Poland" was supported by Catholic radio and websites (especially Radio Maria) in Poland, which also criticize Pope Francis's policy of hospitality toward migrants.

Hungary and Poland have signed an accord with the Czech Republic and Slovakia, the so-called Visegrad Pact, of countries opposed to European solidarity around the distribution of migrants among all the countries within the European Union. Unfortunately Brussels, instead of punishing these governments, is accommodating their policies by rejecting the modification of the Dublin Regulation that would result in a more equitable distribution of migrants.

In Holland, too, the anti-immigrant impulses are very strong. The country's second party, the PVV, led by the Islamophobic Geert Wilders, has, until now, been constrained to the opposition. But even the governments led by Mark Rutte, leader of the liberals (VVD, the Popular Party for Liberty and

Democracy), have displayed strong identity and nationalist thrusts.

In the 2021 elections Holland shifted still further to the right. The party with the most votes was that of the liberals; the VVD of outgoing Premier Rutte had 20 percent of the votes. But it was the extreme right that emerged with strength. With the fall of the Islamophobic Wilders, who came in third, also came the growth of the FVD (Forum for Democracy) of Thierry Bandet and of the new party JA21. Together, these three parties of the extreme right totaled about 18 percent of the votes, a confirmation of how even in Holland the push of white supremacy is very strong.[6]

Also in nearby Denmark, at the beginning of 2021, Parliament voted a law that would permit the transfer abroad of those seeking asylum, to a country not yet specified. Not only that, but the Danish government has begun a series of measures to discourage migrants from entering the country and is now preparing to cut benefits aiding foreigners. Now Denmark is renting prisons in Kosovo to transfer three hundred detainees, a good number of whom are migrants.

Such efforts are likewise appearing in England, above all in the United Kingdom's Independence Party (UKIP), initially led by Nigel Farage, who brought the country to Brexit in 2020. With Farage's exit from the party (2018), the UKIP has gone further to the right, joined by YouTubers of the British alt-right. After the terror attacks at Manchester and London in 2017 there have been fearful increases in aggression against

---

[6] Translator's note: In the November 21, 2023, Dutch elections, the PVV party of Islamophobe Geert Wilders doubled its seats in the Parliament, thereby becoming the largest party in Holland, giving Wilders the opportunity to attempt to organize a coalition government with himself at its head as prime minister.

Muslims. According to the report *State of Hate*, 49 percent of those who vote conservative consider Islam a threat to the British lifestyle.

Also, in Greece there is a notable growth of another party of the extreme right, Golden Dawn, which holds 5–7 percent of the vote. And in the nearby island of Cyprus, in the tracks of Golden Dawn, the ultra-right Elam party won 6.7 percent of support in the elections held on May 30, 2021.

## Italy: "State Racism"

Finally, we turn our eyes to Italy, my own country, which in recent years has seen a dramatic rise of the extreme right. At the political level, it began with Silvio Berlusconi's taking power in 1994 with his party Forza Italia.[7]

Berlusconi articulated well the common thinking of the right, and also of very many Italians. In a press conference held in Berlin on September 26, 2001, he said,

> We cannot put all civilizations on the same level. . . . We must remain conscious of the *superiority of our civilization*. A civilization that has brought a broad well-being in the populations of the countries where it is found. A civilization that guarantees respect for human, religious and political rights. Respect which certainly does not exist in Islamic countries. . . . *The West is destined to continue to westernize and to conquer peoples*." (*Vita*, September 26, 2001)

---

[7] Translator's note: In Italian, *forza* means "force," "strength," or "power"—suggesting "Italy Strong," though it is often translated as an exhortation: "Go Italy!"

In this speech Berlusconi articulates the thinking not only of the right, but also that of many Italian citizens, thinking radicalized by the extreme right of the Lega party of Matteo Salvini and of the Fratelli d'Italia party of Giorgia Meloni.[8]

The Lega party was born at the end of the 1980s under the leadership of Umberto Bossi and continued to grow, showing a deep disdain first for the South, then of the Roma, of Blacks, and above all, of migrants. Once it was in power it, together with the right, expressed the whole of its racism in that "legislative masterpiece" that is the Bossi-Fini Law: an abominable law, beyond immoral, that does not recognize migrants as having any rights, but exist solely as a labor force, leaving them underpaid and, when they are no longer needed, destined to be shipped back home.

Next came the decrees of the then-minister of the interior, Roberto Maroni (Lega party), that are a distillate of pure racism. And then with the first Conte government, supported by the Lega party and by the Five Star Movement,[9] the then-minister of the interior, Salvini, received Parliamentary ap-

---

[8] Translator's note: The word *Lega* means "league." The Lega party, short for Lega Per Salvini Premier (the league for Salvini as premier), began in 2017, and derived its name from a prior rightist party called Lega Nord, or Northern League, formed by six regional parties in 1989 and promoting the secession of the northern regions of Italy. *Fratelli d'Italia* means "Brothers of Italy," which in the September 2022 elections won the highest number of seats in Parliament, resulting in a coalition government that includes Salvini and his Lega party but was led by the Fratelli d'Italia leader, Giorgia Meloni, as Italy's prime minister.

[9] Translator's note: The Five Star Movement was started in 2009 as a nonaligned protest movement by popular Italian comedian Beppe Grillo; it grew in popularity to the extent that it had the most votes in Parliament and was the largest partner of the first Conte government. It played the leading role in two govenments, as well, ruling together for a portion of that time with Salvini's Lega party.

proval of his decrees which introduced principles incompatible with Italian legal culture. Responding, Professor Piero Basso, in his volume *State Racism*, rightly declares that "the legislation on migrants who we have in Italy, in Europe, and in the United States, is really and truly State racism."

The Salvini decrees, a real injury to the European legal order, will, according to Luigi Ferrajoli, "lower the moral sense to the lowest common denominator." In fact, the Salvini decrees brand rescues at sea as criminal. These decrees, according to Luigi Manconi, bring into question

> an irrevocable principle of civil law, that is, mutual aid as a right and duty, which is a foundation of social bonds and marks the passage from isolated individual to community member. In other words, the right of rescue is the first expression of the right to life, upon which the entire system of fundamental rights rests.

And Manconi concludes: "It is urgently necessary to launch a public discussion on the right to rescue as an essential principle of civil law and as a universal right, founded on the law of the sea, and international law."

Those decrees, the expression of a xenophobic culture, ought to have been *repealed*, but instead, with the second Conte government (Five Star, PD, and LEU),[10] they have only been slightly modified. The critical point is that there still remains a monetary fine, even though greatly diminished, for

---

[10] Translator's note: Five Star, with the PD (Partito Democratico, or the Democratic Party) and LEU (Liberi E Uguali, or Free and Equal Party), were the partners constituting the coalition of the second Conte government, formed after Salvini had withdrawn his Lega party's support of the first.

anyone who saves lives at sea, so branding the saving of lives at sea (a basis of all human society) as a crime. This is entirely absurd. The ships of nongovernmental organizations (NGOs) have had to make up for the lack of the functioning constitutional duty of the State: saving human lives!

And so we have before us a Mediterranean Sea that might more aptly be called a Black Sea because it is the cemetery of the "dark" faces.

We do not know how many migrants are buried in that sea, but there are so many. . . . Some sources claim thirty thousand, some sixty thousand. I have the impression that we are now nearing one hundred thousand. One day they will say about us what, today, we say of the Nazis.

Unfortunately, either because it is simply convenient, or because of the constant propaganda of the right and the extreme right, we have become anesthetized to the suffering of others. "How can we not hear the desperate cry of so many brothers and sisters," asked Pope Francis when receiving the refugees of Lesbos, "who prefer to face a stormy sea rather than die slowly in the Libyan concentration camps, places of torture and ignoble slavery? How can we 'pass by,' and thereby make ourselves responsible for their deaths? Our laziness is a sin!"

And it is a crime against humanity.

As the extreme right advances, Lega and Fratelli d'Italia keep repeating to us: "Italians first!" And there are two other parties based on a foundation even more racist and xenophobic. I am speaking of Forza Nuova and Casa Pound,[11] clearly

---

[11] Translator's note: *Forza Nuova* means New Force, and *Casa Pound* means Pound House, an obscure reference which may be to the political leaning of the poet Ezra Pound.

influenced by fascism and nationalism. And they are fed by the European and American extreme right. Forza Nuova finds its roots and support in the English extreme right, while Casa Pound is strongly supported by the party of Marine Le Pen in France. According to the *Guardian,* Forza Nuova receives funds from two English Trusts: St. Michael the Archangel, and St. George Educational.

Casa Pound, whose secretary is Gianluca Iannone, is now a party of six thousand card-carrying members. It is a sinister wave with hundreds of locations, a web radio, book stores, publishing houses, and more. In the space of a few years it has attracted thousands of followers on its social media, public-discussion sites, seats on local councils. And dozens of youth groups, from Azione Studentesca to Blocco Universitario, from Generazione Identitaria to Lotta Studentesca, from Audere Semper to Veneto Fronte Skinheads,[12] linger around the world of the extreme right. A clear example of their work was the assault on the CGIL[13] of Rome on October 9, 2021, led by the extreme right (Forza Nuova and Casa Pound), which insidiously infiltrated an anti-vaccination demonstration. From the investigations it would seem that they were planning an occupation of Palazzo Chigi[14] (similar to the attack on Congress in Washington on January 6, 2021).

---

[12] Translator's note: *Azione Studentesca* means "student action"; *Blocco Universitario* means "university coalition"; *Generazione Identitaria* means "identity generation"; *Lotta Studentesca* means "student struggle"; *Audere Semper* (Latin for "always dare") is a transparent reference to a widely known 1930s Italian fascist slogan. *Veneto Fronte Skinheads* ("Skinheads Front of Veneto") refers to the region immediately around Venice.

[13] Translator's note: CGIL is the Italian General Confederation of Labor, Italy's oldest and largest trade union.

[14] Translator's note: Palazzo Chigi, in Rome, as both the seat of the Italian Council of Ministers and the official residence of the prime minister,

Among those investigated for the attack on CGIL, still in custody are Roberto Fiore, founder of Forza Nuova, and Giuliano Castellino, leader of Forza Nuova at Rome.[15] In this country the right and the extreme right are a powerful force that the Italian people are befriending.

A survey by the Pew Research Center in 2017 found that Italy has the largest number of voters who claim a populist orientation: 38 percent. In Italy, too, the middle class fears losing its wealth and wants to preserve it by stopping what it considers the "invasion" of the "refuse" of the world. That is why it votes with the "populist wave" of the right.

"This new populism," Luigi Ferrajoli rightly affirms in the November 20, 2020, edition of *il manifesto,*

> has in this manner resulted in, and continues to result in, in addition to deaths at sea, grave damage to the basis of society and the ideals of our democracy: the lowering of a moral sense, and of the public spirit, in the popular culture. When indifference to suffering and death, when inhumanity, and immoral slogans such as "Italians first," used to justify the omission of rescues, are practiced and displayed by institutions, they are not only legitimized, but also welcomed and nourished.

---

is the headquarters of the executive branch of the Italian government.

[15] Translator's note: On December 20, 2023, the Rome trial court sentenced Fiore, Castellano, and three others to more than eight years imprisonment each; they vowed to appeal. News reports recounted that the sentence was met by shouts in the courtroom, "We will never give up," and the Roman salute by spectators. The *Saluto Romano* (Roman salute) is an extended-arm gesture that was adopted by Mussolini in Italy in the 1920s, followed soon after by the Nazis in Germany.

They become contagious and normalized. Without this corruption of our moral sense, brought about by the display of immorality by the heads of state, we would not understand the mass consent that was enjoyed by fascism, and which is enjoyed today, in their countries, by Trump, Bolsonaro, Orban and Erdogan. They have sown fear and hate for those who are different. They have turned communal feeling into fascism. They have discredited, by the denunciation of those who save human lives, the practice of rescue of those whose lives are in danger, and, with it, the normal human sentiments that form the assumptions of democracy.

"The far right," reports *The New York Times,* "has become the new normal in Europe." And it goes on: "The recurring themes of the alt-right have become the common position of many parties, and they now make up part of the political center." There are groups that promote the persecution of minorities, nationalism, and racism. They fear the substitution of white Europeans with other ethnicities, as well as the growth of the feared "Eurabia": an "Islamicized" continent. The father of this theory is the seventy-four year old Frenchman Renaud Camus, author of the book *Grand Replacement*. His thesis is that the European peoples will become replaced by Arabic Muslim peoples. Camus is running in the next European Union elections, and among the stated aims of his platform is: "It is not necessary to leave the European Union, but to make Africa (which colonizes it) leave *it*: we must fight against replacement." With words like these he has inspired many racist claims on the internet.

We are facing an international sinister wave. "It is a sort of reactionary 'Internationale,'"[16] denounces Professor Steven Forti,

> which reunites the aristocracy of radical conservatism with the ultra-right on a global scale. Anyone who still thinks the new ultra-right is a national phenomenon, or is limited to a few countries, is seriously mistaken. It is worth pointing out again: the extreme right 2.0 is a great family with transatlantic ties and a plethora of think tanks, foundations, institutes, and associations which, in the last two decades, have spun a thick web that promotes a shared agenda, besides moving huge sums of money.

Daniel Lombroso, the director of the documentary *White Noise*, asserts:

> I have discovered two things; first, that White nationalism exerts an enormous attraction among the young, the world over (in the USA, but obviously also in Italy, France, Russia and elsewhere); second, that these ideas are similar to drugs: they make you feel powerful, but the persons pushing them are profoundly alienated, narcissistic, and depressed.

---

[16] Translator's note: The Internationale began as the International Workingman's Association in England in 1864, and over succeeding decades it and its successors became associated with left and radical left political positions. "The Internationale" is also the title of the song it adopted as its anthem.

## "Lone Wolves"?

The web has significantly favored the growth of the extreme right. The welding of "extreme ideology and the use of the internet as a means of spreading propaganda is extremely dangerous," say the Carabinieri of the ROS[17] who investigate on the web. And Christopher Wray, director of the FBI, stated before a committee of the House of Representatives that political violence of the extreme right is a "top threat to the national security." As dangerous as ISIS. The commander of ROS, General Pasquale Angelosanto, has asserted: "We are alert to the phenomenon, and we are paying particular attention to 'white supremacy' which supports the domination of the white race over others." He maintains that "the internet, social networks, and online channels represent a great uniting instrument that joins bad actors by a common thread of shared ideology."

These sites are numerous in Italy, too, and they show up on Telegram as Il Sole Nero, Fascio Littorio, Hyperborean World View, Fascismo V2–LGBTshit, Avanguardia Nazionale Socialista, Meridiano Zero.[18] On Sole Nero we find a

---

[17] Translator's note: The Carabinieri are a branch of the Italian government's military, who are charged with police investigative work. One of its branches is the ROS (Raggruppamento Operativo Speciale, or Special Operations Group), which investigates terrorism, organized crime, and other criminal activity.

[18] Translator's note: *Sole Nero* means "black sun," a symbol with a Nazi past; *Fascio Littorio* means "Lictor's Bundle," a reference to an ancient Roman phrase adopted by Italian fascists in the 1930s; *Hyperborean* is a reference to the peoples of the far north of the globe; *Fascismo* means "fascism"; *Avanguardia Nazionale Socialista* means "national socialist vanguard" (a name similar to the official name of the German Nazi party, National Socialist German Workers' Party; *Meridiano Zero* means "the zero—or prime—meridian."

strong Nazi cabalism with swastikas and photos of Hitler with actual calls for race war. On Meridiano Zero we find also Holocaust denial, and on Fascismo V2–LGBTshit insults and threats against gays, Blacks, Jews, and others.

Some Italian supremacists, besides those on Telegram, appear on the Russian social media Vkontakte, where neo-Nazis banned by Facebook also reappear. This site is a den of neo-fascists looking for followers.

In an interview on L'Espresso, General Angelosanto further affirms, "The new generation of extremists, by resorting to the web, has found a swift channel of communication, immediate, and free from every form of control." It feeds the concept of white supremacy and the idea that the Aryan race must not be contaminated by Jews and Blacks.

It is here that the so-called lone wolves are nourished and connected; they are not really so solitary, because they are supported by Nazi-fascist groups, sustained in their turn by parties of the extreme right.

The first of the "lone wolves" to take action was the Norwegian Anders Breivik. On July 22, 2011, he accomplished the slaughter of sixty-eight youths gathered at a youth camp on the Island of Utoya in Norway.

From acts such as these spring copycats. A few months later, on December 13, there was a slaughter in Florence, right in the center of the city: two Senegalese migrants, Samb Modou and Diop Mor, were killed by an extremist of the right, a supporter of Casa Pound, Gianluca Casseri, who killed himself to avoid arrest.

Another "lone wolf," David Sonboly, a German eighteen year old of Iranian origin, on July 22, 2016, killed nine persons in the Olympic commercial center of Monaco. On

February 3, 2018, at Macerata, there was a racist attack where Luca Traini, a twenty-eight-year-old member of Lega and an admirer of Hitler, shot from his auto while driving through several sections of the city, wounding six persons, all Africans, guilty of having black skin, like the murderer of poor Pamela Mastropietro. When Traini was arrested, he gave the Roman salute.

On May 13, 2019, the supremacist Brenton Tarrant at Christchurch in New Zealand killed forty-nine Muslims who were praying in two mosques and injured another forty-eight. Traini's name was written on the rifle that Tarrant used. Before undertaking this horrendous act, he had posted his manifesto on the internet: "The genocide of the Whites, caused by mass immigration."

On September 28 of the same year, in El Paso, Texas, American Patrick Crusius killed twenty-two people, wounding another twenty-four. With the same messages of hate found on Tarrant's social-media post, he wrote, "I defend my country from ethnic and cultural substitution, carried out by an invasion." A few days later, on October 9, there was an anti-Semitic attack. Stephan Balliet, twenty-eight years old, an extremist of the right, during the Jewish observance of Yom Kippur, assaulted the synagogue in Halle, Germany, where fifty-two faithful were gathered. Unable to enter, he killed two random passersby and a young man of twenty years in a nearby diner. Beforehand, he had published a document in which he affirmed that "the root of all the problems are the Jews," then adding, "the objective of States is to kill the greatest number of anti-Whites, better if they are Jews."

It seems that, in Germany alone, there are more than twelve thousand people belonging to neo-Nazi groups. And these groups are often armed. In Germany, another massacre of nine foreigners also took place at Hanau on February 20, 2020. The "lone wolf" also died, having written, "Some people that cannot be expelled from Germany will be exterminated." In 2020 alone, three neo-fascist groups were disbanded who were prepared for armed battle.

Returning to Italy, our country, I would like to underscore the January 22, 2021, arrest of Andrea Cavalleri, a twenty-two year old from Savona. He wanted to imitate Anders Breivik and Brenton Tarrant, motivated by a supremacist ideology. He planned to accomplish his slaughters by means of his group, The New Social Order, which propagandized on the Telegram channel Sole Nero. He is accused of collaborating with others with the goal of terrorism and of encouraging massacres in schools. "I'll pull off a slaughter, for sure. The only thing to do is die fighting. I have the weapons. I will be Traini 2.0." Not only Jews were targeted; the Savona youth had also targeted women. "The Jews are only the first evil to be eliminated." On that day there would be twelve searches of persons tied to the young twenty-two year old in the cities of Genoa, Turin, Cagliari, Forli, Cesena, Palermo, Perugia, Bologna, and Cuneo. This is the clearest demonstration of how extensive the phenomenon of the extreme right is, and that of white supremacy, even in my country.

The drift toward neo-Nazism in Europe is now a reality, and Italy is no exception. In November of 2019 the prosecutor's office of Caltanisetta uncovered the existence of an Italian National Socialist Party of Workers[19] of Nazi, xenophobic, and anti-Semitic ilk, with many symbols taken from the

---

[19] Translator's note: That is the exact formal name (except for the country), of the Gerrman Nazi Party.

Waffen-SS; they were furnished with weapons and explosives and had branches in Lombardy, Piedmont, Liguria, and Veneto. A few days prior, the DIGOS[20] of Florence had conducted searches of twelve people accused of subverting the democratic order, finding German weapons from the Nazi era, as well as explosives, and uniforms. The group had intended to create a "republican national guard called up to intervene, with weapons in hand." In mid-July of 2019, near Voghera at Rivanazzano, DIGOS tracked down a huge arsenal of the extreme right containing air-to-air missiles. "It is domestic terrorism," commented the journalist Michele Serra,

> with a full stomach and a poisoned brain which celebrates extermination as the inevitable outcome of the unworthiness, the inferiority, the non-belonging to the human race of the Jews, the Africans, the Muslims, to whom must be added, according to the would-be slaughterer of Savona, also women.

The latest investigation, of May 2021, coordinated by the Prosecutor's Office of Aquila, resulted in a series of searches in different regions of Italy, revealing an organization called the Last Legion, which demonstrated a high degree of violent fanaticism, soaked with xenophobia and Naziphile nostalgia, with the intention of overturning the democratic order. It operates mainly in Lombardy and Abruzzo (especially in Aquila, Pescara, and Chieti). On the Vkontakte platform it posted a video in which it declares that one of the members

---

[20] Translator's note: "DIGOS" stands for Divisione Investigazioni Generali Ed Operazioni Speciali (Division of General Investigations and Special Operations) and is a branch of the police.

had formed a party with the "antidemocratic goals proper to the Fascist Party." Very active on social media, the twenty-five persons investigated mocked the "values of the Constitution," with homophobic and anti-migrant posts.

The great question is: Is there a cause-effect relationship between the ideology of white supremacy and the daily episodes of racism against Black and brown faces in our country? Based on what happens daily in Italy directed at Black people, the short answer is "Yes." The number of aggressions in our country targeting Black or Roma people is astounding. From the murder of the Malian laborer and trade unionist Soumaila Sacko, twenty-nine years old, guilty of collecting, together with his friends, some pieces of sheet metal from an abandoned factory in the Province of Vibo in order to build shacks for themselves, to the youth of twenty-one years from Cape Verde, William Monteiro Duarte, beaten to death at Colleferro by a group of young neo-fascists.

It is a long and weighty list of aggressions, both verbal and physical, against Blacks, Roma, Jews, and anyone not part of the white world. The support of soccer fans, in recent times, has become a pure exercise in the verbal attack against Black and other minorities. It is even more unbelievable to see the racist torrent that runs across the internet, which has now become a garbage can for depositing pure slime. And who can forget the river of insults that an Auschwitz survivor, the Jewish Senator Liliana Segre, received, hurled at her out of racial hatred?

# 5

# Toward a Pluralistic Humanity

## Embarrassing Questions

We must look the supremacy of the White Tribe in the face to see how it is closing in on itself, to defend its identity, its lifestyle, and its sense of privilege.

How can we escape from this situation? "If we wish to understand the world in which we live, we must see it as a whole and not just from our own point of view," asserts Tiziano Terzani, a great journalist and even greater thinker who allowed himself be "converted" by the peoples he had encountered in Asia. "The problem is that as long as we think we have a monopoly on the good," he writes in his book *Letters against the War*, published in 2001 on the eve of the invasion of Afghanistan, "as long as we speak only of our own civilization, ignoring that of others, we will not be on the right path."

Another Italian journalist who permitted himself to be touched by the "other" is Andrea Nicastro of the *Corriere*

Della Sera,[1] who, in his book *We Are the Other*, relates how his own "conversion" came about. Nicastro invites Westerners to look at our history as "the Muslim peoples may see it." He discusses the colonial occupation of Dar al-Islam,[2] the house of Islam, which still weighs like a millstone on the Islamic psyche. He also focuses on the relations between the West and Islam from 1950 to today, a period characterized by homicidal wars against Islamic countries such as Chechnya, Iran, Lebanon, Afghanistan, Iraq, Libya, and Syria, causing millions of deaths and destroying entire nations. The rich North, armed to the teeth to protect its wealth and its privileges, brought war to "rogue states," to the "axis of evil," according to US President George W. Bush, with the cry of "God is near." His war against Iraq, above all the rest, was perceived by the Muslims as the war of the Western Christian against Islam.

This gave birth to jihad, which took different forms and appearance in different countries: al Qaeda, ISIS, Boko Haram, Shabab, and others. Nicastro maintains that jihad uses Islam as an ideological cover, but that the jihadists are moved by a strong feeling of "global payback for injustice." Nicastro poses the question to us as Westerners: "Why not take action against the origin of the problem (inequality) instead of its symptom (terrorism)?"

That is an embarrassing question for us Westerners who persist in fighting jihadists in wars that become ever more dreadful. The 2003 war against Iraq, which Nicastro saw as a reporter, is just one example. This war, completely built

---

[1] Translator's note: *Corriere Della Sera* (the evening messenger) is a major daily newspaper published in Milan, Italy.

[2] Translator's note: Dar al-Islam is an Islamic term for the Muslim regions of the world.

on lies, caused half a million deaths, cost the United States 3 trillion dollars (according to an estimate by the economist Joseph Stiglitz), and was the "mother of ISIS" (according to then-US President Obama).

Nicastro then goads the Western churches with a weighty accusation: it is "Islam as loser, not Christianity as winner, which is the source of suffering that carries with it a nostalgia for an ancient order as a reaction to a consciousness of what is perceived as more unjust, unequal, and violent because it was based solely on money."

And yet Christianity is inspired by Jesus, who took upon himself the suffering of his people and challenged the imperial Roman system in league with the Temple that oppressed his people, a challenge launching the kingdom of God, a dream of a world more human and more fraternal. It was for this that Jesus was crucified by the Roman Empire as a troublemaker; crucifixion was used by the Romans for slaves and rebels, among others. And the followers of Jesus, for the first three centuries, were seen as dangerous to the order of the Caesars and were therefore persecuted. The book of the Apocalypse, in its symbolic language, describes the Roman Empire as the most horrible beast to ever arise from the Mediterranean Sea.

But after Constantine, the churches became imperial, intertwined with both the Western and Eastern empires. And as we have seen, the churches in the West have played a key role in the conquest of Latin America, bringing European imperialism, even as there remained prophetic voices, remembering Jesus, who have fought against prevailing injustices.

Still, to this day the churches of the West are part of the "empire of money," which kills by hunger and by wars, rendering the planet more unlivable for humankind, an empire that has now become the most ferocious beast that walks the planet.

By good fortune we today have a pope like Francis, who has written extensively about the "wrong path" that so much of humanity is on; his texts merit careful consideration by the entire White Tribe, including all secularists of good will—not just adherents of the Catholic faith—regarding what it means to bring about its "conversion," leading us to the entrance onto the "right path" toward a more pluralistic humanity.

Pope Francis has had the courage to say that we are not within Christianity, not anymore! challenging the church to become poor again, as Jesus Christ envisioned it, a poor church standing alongside those who are the least, a church capable of shouting out the suffering of humanity, and prepared to become outcast and persecuted for doing so. In his apostolic exhortation *Evangelii Gaudium*; in his two encyclicals *Laudato Si'* and *Fratelli Tutti*; and in his speeches to the participants in the World Meeting(s) of Popular Movements (WMPM),[3] Pope Francis has courageously launched an alternative project to that of the Empire of Mammon. At the third World Meeting of Popular Movements in 2016, he asked:

> What governs then? Money. How does it govern? With the whip of fear, of inequality, of economic, social, cultural and military violence, which spawns ever greater violence in a seemingly unending downward spiral. So much pain and so much fear!

---

[3] Translator's note: *Evangelii Gaudium* is Latin for "The Joy of the Gospel," *Laudato Si'* and *Fratelli Tutti* (both Italian, and both quoting directly the words of St. Francis), mean "Praise Be to You," and "Brothers All." In the first line of *Fratelli Tutti*, Pope Francis explains that the title refers to *all* of us, declaring, "With these words, Saint Francis of Assisi addressed his *brothers and sisters*."

He goes on,

> There is . . . a basic terrorism that is born of the overall control of money worldwide and strikes at humanity as a whole. That basic terrorism feeds derivative forms of terrorism like narcoterrorism, state terrorism and what some wrongly term ethnic or religious terrorism, even though no people, no religion, is terrorist. Certainly, there are small fundamentalist groups on all sides. But terrorism begins when you drive out the marvel of creation, man and woman, and put money in their place. That system is terroristic.

## A Cultural and Ethical Revolution

That is how Pope Francis overturns a Western "omelette-like" conception of terrorism, reminding us that the primary terrorism is the economic-financial-military system that "ever creates more violence." In 2013 Pope Francis wrote in *Evangelii Gaudium*: "Such an economy kills." And two years later, in the encyclical *Laudato Si'*, he asserted that economy kills not only people, but also the entire planet:

> This sister [our sister, Mother Earth][4] now cries out to us because of the harm we have inflicted on her by our irresponsible use and abuse of the goods with which God has endowed her. We have come to see ourselves as her lords and masters, entitled to plunder her at will.

---

[4] Translator's note: The encyclical had referred to the earth with this term and in these exact words, in its previous paragraph, using the words of St. Francis of Assisi.

How can we escape from this situation? In his encyclical *Fratelli Tutti*, as Raniero La Valle[5] explains in his article "Papa Francesco indica l'ultima carta per cambiare il paradigm dell'umano" in *il manifesto,* the pontiff "tells us that we need to change the *model of the human*," that is, "to pass from a *society of 'associates'* to a *community of brothers*," if we want to save ourselves. "This is an encyclical about love," according to La Valle, "because to pass from associates to sons[6] means to pass from the search for the useful, to that of love, with no reason."

Unfortunately, our Western societies have become a means of capitalistic production. In this system we are used and then thrown away. "We have created a throwaway culture," Pope Francis writes in *Evangelii Gaudium*, a culture

> which is now spreading. It is no longer simply about exploitation and oppression, but something new. Exclusion ultimately has to do with what it means to be a part of the society in which we live; those excluded are no longer society's underside or its fringes or its disenfranchised—they are no longer even a part of it. The excluded are not the "exploited," but the outcast, the "leftovers."

---

[5] Translater's note: La Valle is a noted Italian intellectual, journalist, and politician, one of whose writings, in 2016, was the Manifesto of "Catholics for No" on a constitutional referendum. One of its first signers was Alex Zanotelli.

[6] Translator's note: The quoted La Valle article (in Italian) speaks of the pope, in this encyclical, as adopting the role of a father speaking to his children, who, therefore, being all sons (and daughters) of the same father, are, thus, "brothers (and sisters), all." That is (in Italian) *Fratelli Tutti*.

What Pope Francis asks of humanity, instead, is a *cultural revolution*: passing from a society of "associates" to a community of brothers. La Valle writes:

> This is an encyclical for secularists (or rather for extraordinary secularists), because love does not allow itself to be ensnared within any one time, in any one approach, in any single text. . . . Pluralism is always invoked, not relativism, always with enthusiasm for differences, for the unknown, for what is not yet understood; the figure with many faces, not the Babel from the tower of claims of homogeneity!

To arrive at such a community of brothers, Pope Francis asserts in *Fratelli Tutti*, we must practice not only *individual* charity, but above all, *political* charity:

> For whereas individuals can help others in need, when they join together in initiating social processes of fraternity and justice for all, they enter the "field of charity at its most vast, namely political charity." This entails working for a social and political order whose soul is social charity. Once more, I appeal for a renewed appreciation of politics as a "lofty vocation and one of the highest forms of charity, inasmuch as it seeks the common good."

And Francis also tells us that "politics must not be subject to the economy" (and, I would add, must not be subject to the world of finance). The dream of Francis is

> a truly human and fraternal society . . . capable of ensuring, in an efficient and stable way that each of its

members is accompanied, at every stage of life. Not only by providing for their basic needs, but by enabling them to give the best of themselves, even though their performance may be less than optimum, their pace slow or their efficiency limited.

To bring about this dream, Pope Francis calls into question three taboos of the present system: *private property, just war,* and the *death penalty*. Pope Francis says that the "the principle of the common use of created goods is the first principle of the whole ethical and social order," so that "the right to private property can only be considered a secondary natural right, derived from the principle of the universal destination of created goods." Francis draws two direct important consequences from this consideration: "Development must not aim at the amassing of wealth by a few, but must ensure human rights—personal and social, economic and political, including the rights of nations and of peoples."

Later, he applies this principle of the "universal destination" of goods to the drama of the refugees: "Each country also belongs to the foreigner, inasmuch as a territory's goods must not be denied to a needy person coming from elsewhere."

The second taboo that Pope Francis calls into question is the theology of the "just war" elaborated by St. Augustine (430 AD) and taught by the church over the ages. With nuclear and biological weapons of mass destruction, "it is very difficult nowadays to invoke the rational criteria elaborated in earlier centuries to speak of the possibility of a 'just war.' *Never again war!*" The third taboo called into question is that of the death penalty inflicted by the state. "Today we state clearly that the death penalty is inadmissible and the Church is firmly committed to calling for its abolition worldwide."

Pope Francis is radicalizing the teaching of the Catholic Church on these three fundamental issues in order to make possible the construction of a "society of brothers." But to realize this, it is the church itself that must "be converted," that must "change course." Few have expressed this dream so well as an old friend of mine, the Jesuit Silvano Fausti, in his last book, his testament, *Sogni, Allergie, Benedizioni* (dreams, allergies, and blessings)[7]:

> I dream of a pope who convenes a council,
> Not a "Third Vatican,"
> But a "Second of Jerusalem,"[8]
> To "de-religion-ize" the church
> In the sense of Barth,[9]
> Or at least to "de-clerical-ize" it
> In the Catholic sense
> Or at least to "de-Roman-ize" it
> In the gospel's sense
> Or at least to "de-cultural-ize" it
> In the etymological "apostolic" sense.

This is the testament of a man who has worked in the outskirts of Milan (Villa Pizzone) but remained in constant contact with the outskirts of the world, Africa most of all. It may also be the dream of Pope Francis, himself a Jesuit like Fausti.

---

[7] Silvano Fausti, *Sogni, Allergie, Benedizioni*, 2013, Edizioni San Paolo, Balsamo, Italy.

[8] Translator's note: The Council of Jerusalem is a council described in chap. 15 of the Acts of the Apostles, thought to have been held in Jerusalem in about 48–50 A.D.

[9] Translator's note: Karl Barth (1886–1968) was a theologian whose far-reaching influence extended well beyond his Swiss Reformed Church background.

One thing is clear: The church has for centuries been an integral part of the various systems that have governed the world. This is the opposite of what is commanded by Jesus in Mark's Gospel: "It shall not be so among you," he said, rejecting the request of the disciples James and John when they requested positions of authority at the time Jesus would come into his kingdom.

> You know that those who are supposed to rule over the Gentiles lord it over them, and their great men exercise authority over them. But it shall not be so among you; but whoever would be great among you must be your servant, and whoever would be first among you must be the slave of all. (10:42–44)

That is why there must be a radical reform of the central structures of the Catholic Church, which are the relic of centuries in which the church was a political power. By the Second Vatican Council many bishops already sought such radical reform. One of them was the Archbishop of Recife (Brazil), Dom Hélder Câmara. After the council Dom Hélder wrote a letter to Pope Paul VI in which he proposed that, to accomplish his mission with greater freedom with respect to the world powers,

> the Pope should return to being the bishop of Rome and Primate of the Churches in the West. He should return to residence in the Lateran Palace, the ancient papal residence at Rome, renouncing his role as head of state, leaving the Vatican to become an international museum—thus eliminating papal nuncios (the Pope

ought not to have diplomats to the various national governments) and communicating with countries instead, by way of local bishops.

Dom Hélder did not receive a response from Paul VI, but he received a letter from the secretary of state, Cardinal Villot, which stated, in part: "His Excellency must understand that we no longer live in Gospel times."

But a radical reform of the Vatican still remains today a fundamental step if the church wishes to realize the dream of Pope Francis, which he has expressed so well in the encyclical *Fratelli Tutti* and in the *Document on Human Fraternity* that followed it.

The *Document on Human Fraternity* signed by Pope Francis and by the Grand Imam of Al-Azhar, Ahmad Al-Tayyib, on February 4, 2019, represents a step forward in the encounter between Christians and Muslims, one of enormous importance. The fundamental passage of the document is this:

> Freedom is a right of every person: each individual enjoys the freedom of belief, thought, expression and action. The pluralism and the *diversity of religions*, colour, sex, race and language are *willed by God in His wisdom*, through which He created human beings. This divine wisdom is the source from which the right to freedom of belief and the *freedom to be different derives*.[10] Therefore, the fact that people are forced to adhere to a certain religion or culture must be rejected, as too the imposition of a cultural way of life that others do not accept.

---

[10] Emphasis added by Alex Zanotelli.

The theologian Carlo Molari writes:

> Let us remember "willed by God in His wisdom" as the source of pluralism of religions, and that the *Document* justifies, *de jure*,[11] the diversity and multiplicity of religion inasmuch as it is a *good*, even if imperfect, and not as an evil. As a matter of evolutionary perspective, we can say that the variety of religions is not due to sin or to the ignorance of mankind, but to the divine Wisdom.

## Reparations When?

Entering onto the path laid out by Pope Francis will not be easy for either the West or for the church. The West (and the White Tribe) would have to accept its grave historical responsibility both for the extermination of the aboriginal peoples of North America, South America, and Australia, as well as for the enslavement of the Black peoples and for the colonial conquest of the peoples of the Global South. A filthy history of violence, oppression, depredations, exterminations, and genocides of millions of human beings. Was this not, perhaps, the most dreadful Holocaust in human history?

The West should first publicly recognize its responsibility for the massacres and genocides that it brought about. A prime example of doing this was the action taken by the Catholic Church, when, in the Jubilee Year of 2000, Pope John Paul II asked pardon for the misdeeds of the church beginning with the Crusades and the Inquisition:

"We cannot allow," Pope Francis asserts in *Fratelli Tutti*,

---

[11] Translaters note: *De jure* is Latin for "as a matter of law."

present and future generations to lose the memory of what happened. It is a memory that ensures and encourages the building of a more fair and fraternal future. Neither must we forget the persecutions, the slave trade and the ethnic killings that continue . . . that make us ashamed of our humanity.

But this important first step must be followed by the remedy for the harm done. This remedy was forcefully insisted on by Nobel Peace Prize–laureate Desmond Tutu, president of the Truth and Reconciliation Commission, established by the president of free South Africa, Nelson Mandela, for reconciliation between Black South Africans and South African whites who were guilty of horrible crimes against Black people during the apartheid regime.

"If we are going to move on and build a new kind of world community," says Desmond Tutu in his book *No Future without Forgiveness*,[12]

> there must be a way in which we can deal with a sordid past. The most effective way would be for the perpetrators or their descendants to acknowledge the awfulness of what happened and the descendants of the victims to respond by granting forgiveness, providing something can be done, even symbolically, to compensate for the anguish experienced, whose consequences are still being lived through today.

And he adds,

---

[12] Desmond Mpilo Tutu, *No Future without Forgiveness* (New York: Doubleday, Image Books, 1999, 2000), 278–79.

It may be, for instance, that race relations in the United States will not improve significantly until Native Americans and African Americans get the opportunity to tell their stories and reveal the pain that sits in the pit of their stomachs as a baneful legacy of dispossession and slavery. We saw in the Truth and Reconciliation Commission how the act of telling one's story has a cathartic, healing effect.

This is a fundamental first step. "True forgiveness," insists Tutu,

> deals with the past, to make the future possible. We cannot go on nursing grudges even vicariously for those who cannot speak for themselves any longer. We have to accept that what we do, we do for generations past, present, and yet to come. That is what makes a community a community or a people a people—for better or worse.

Tepid efforts are under way in some countries. In the United States a commission has been created to study and develop proposals for reparation to African Americans, to discuss the eventual implementation of policies of compensation to the descendants of slaves. In the United States the requests for reparation for slavery are at the center of a lively debate, with dissent even among African Americans.

On this issue the Jesuits of the United States and Canada are giving a good example in their decision to create a fund of $100 million to compensate the descendants of the men and women directly enslaved by Jesuits. *The New York Times* was the newspaper that first revealed that the first Jesuit university, Georgetown University, had been financed through slave labor on Maryland plantations, and then saved from bankruptcy in 1838 by the sale of 272 enslaved people for $115,000 (in today's dollars, $3,000,000). Let us hope that other religious orders and other churches imitate this example.

In France, too, the debate over reparations started in 1998, primarily due to the occasion of the one hundred fiftieth anniversary of the abolition of slavery, and with the Taubira law of 2001, which declared the slave trade and slavery crimes against humanity. France seemed to be at the vanguard in this effort, but then, for various reasons, the push diminished. Germany, which has recently admitted the genocide of the Herero and Nama peoples in Namibia, nevertheless, as I've noted, denies reparations to their descendants.

The only country that has actually taken a step forward is Canada. The government of Justin Trudeau has undertaken an agreement in principle that provides a record compensation to natives of $40 billion in Canadian dollars, destined, in part, to compensate Native children taken from the custody of their families and "entrusted" to the state.

When will my country, Italy, decide to admit the crimes committed in Ethiopia and in Libya and make reparations? The ignorance that exists in my country about the horrors committed by Italian colonialism in Africa is unbelievable. How is it possible that this history is not taught in the public schools? It is because we continue to believe in the myth: "Italians, good people." And we continue to claim that the Italians in Africa have done nothing but good. When will there be a serious debate about reparations? But above all, when will there be a serious foreign policy toward our former colonies: Eritrea, Ethiopia, Somalia, and Libya (all of which are nations that find themselves in the gravest conditions, both political and economic)?

In Italy, couldn't a first step in realizing this dream be the enacting of a law of *jus soli*?[13] It would mean giving life, dignity, and hope to over a million children and young people born in Italy from immigrant parents, and it would be an excellent antidote to the growing racism in this country. This is one road to realizing, in Italy, the dream of the "*conviviality of differences.*"

## And What of Contemporary Disasters?

But it is not just the past that must be remedied; so, too, must the present. Today the White Tribe continues to maintain a combination of economic, financial, and militarized structures that kill by starvation and war, also poisoning the environment. And we do not even notice.

I believe that, in reality, the most effective reparation that the White Tribe could now make is welcoming migrants.

This is the thesis of the Indian American writer Saketu Mehta in his recent book *This Land Is Our Land*. Mehta calculates the value of the silver looted over the centuries by Europe in Latin America at $165 trillion. But "it would be crazy to think that Europe would repay $165 trillion," he stated in an interview published by *La Republica*:

---

[13] Translator's note: *Jus Soli* is a Latin phrase meaning "the law of the land, soil, or ground," which is generally understood to include citizenship in the land of one's birth, or "birthright citizenship."

To wash away this debt it would be sufficient to let the migrants enter. Europe is displaying a rate of growth below the level of fertility. The lowest is Italy's. But even those who do not emigrate would benefit, thanks to the funds sent back home. The increase of the income of those who do emigrate is the best way to help the poor of the world, because the funds remitted home will go to their families, while currently foreign aid from nation states goes to the corrupt local elites. And the funds sent back home are four times the amount of the aid; it is the poor who help the poor. I do not seek open borders, but open hearts.

Only immigration can save Europe, the United States, Canada, and Australia from the catastrophic drop in the rate of demographic growth.

That is why the words of US Vice President Kamala Harris in Guatemala are unacceptable, "Do not come! Do not come!"—words spoken to stop the caravans of the impoverished moving toward the United States, which is directly responsible for the Latin American disaster. We expected better from President Biden.

And the policies of Brussels are also unacceptable—the externalization of the European Union's borders to Turkey, Greece, Libya, Tunisia, and Morocco, to keep the migrants as far away as possible from us.

Unacceptable, too, are the draconian migrant policies of Australia implemented to stop the migrants from Southeast Asia.

A splendid means the White Tribe has for reparation is that of accepting the impoverished who knock on our doors.

That will force the White Tribe to take another fundamental step: recognizing the "other" as benefit and wealth for me, because different from me, at the level of both culture and religion. And this is the great dream: humanity seated at the same table in equal dignity, in deep respect for diversities of culture and religion. The remarkable Bishop of Molfetta, "Father" Tonino Bello, called this *"the conviviality of differences."* Either the world follows this path, or we will tear each other to pieces.

And this is the most difficult challenge for the White Tribe, precisely because it has always considered itself superior to other cultures and religions. The White Tribe conquered and colonized the world with the supposition that it had *civilization, culture,* and *religion.* It will be particularly difficult for us to welcome the Muslim, whom we have battled for a millennium, from the Crusades to the Battle of Lepanto, from the colonial occupation of the Muslim world to the war in Iraq. On both sides the distrust, the suspicion, and even the hatred, are open and obvious.

Still today the relations between these two worlds remain tense, thanks also to the fear-motivated advance of the extreme right, which maintains that Islam is trying to create "Eurabia": the racist theory that holds there is a conspiracy to replace the European population with a Muslim one from North Africa. The extreme right and European populism see in Islam the great enemy that needs to be defeated. In such a situation, it will not be easy for it to encounter the "other," above all, the Muslim.

## And the Churches?

But it will be just as difficult for the Western churches to encounter the "other," especially the Muslim. Indeed, just as Western societies are permeated with the populism of the extreme right, so too are churches in the West permeated by strong fundamentalist movements. This is a phenomenon found in all the world's great religions today, whether Judaism, Hinduism, Islam, or even Buddhism (just look to the hatred on the part of Myanmar's Buddhists toward the Rohingya refugees, who are Muslim). The same fundamentalism is frightfully growing in the Western churches. We see its massive presence in the evangelical churches in the United States, which are expanding into Latin America, and, to some extent, into the entire world. These churches reject the "other" and support the white universe of the extreme right.

Even in the Catholic Church this phenomenon is growing stronger, in the United States, Europe, Australia, and now even among the white Catholics of Latin America. In the Vatican itself there are high prelates such as American Cardinal Raymond Burke and the ex-papal nuncio at Washington, Archbishop Carlo Maria Vigano, who support the ultraconservative wing of the Roman curia and oppose Pope Francis's open route to the "other."[14]

Vigano repeatedly attacked Pope Francis, even calling on him to resign. He also wrote a letter to the then-US President

---

[14] Translator's note: On November 28, 2023, a major news outlet, Reuters, reported that an anonymous "senior Vatican official" had quoted the pope as saying that Burke was "working against the church and against the papacy" and that he had sown "disunity" in the church.

Trump. "I dare to think," he wrote, "that we two are on the same side in this battle, although with different weapons." Vigano was just as insistent regarding COVID-19: "The Green Pass[15] is the mark of Satan."

Cardinal Burke is the president of the Consultative Committee of the Institute of Human Dignity, a think tank of conservative Catholicism whose founding father is Rocco Buttiglione of Community and Liberation. In 2014 the Institute hosted Steve Bannon, a close advisor to Trump, at a Skype meeting, during which he espoused his ultraconservative vision of the world.

Trump, after being elected president, fired Bannon from the White House. Bannon then began touring Europe, solidifying relationships with ultraconservative movements, from Orban in Hungary to Marine Le Pen in France, from the Lega in Italy to many other nationalist movements of Europe. His aim is to create a grand alliance of movements of the ultra-right of the Old Continent, which he has called "The Movement," with headquarters at Brussels. Together with the Institute of Human Dignity, Bannon is trying to acquire the Certosa of Trisulti, near Rome, to turn it into an "Academy for the Judeo-Christian West," to provide training courses founded on the populist view of the universe.

So far, he has not succeeded in acquiring the abbey, but Bannon is not giving up and intends to open this center in Rome or elsewhere. Bannon certainly has the support of the ultra-right, both Catholic and evangelical, in the United

---

[15] Translator's note: *Il Green Pass*, a term adopted in Italian, was part of a system of limited permissions to travel during the total lockdown of the severest early days of the COVID-19 pandemic in Italy, where it had struck first in Europe and with the greatest mortality.

States, in making war on Pope Francis. And it is a ferocious war, this war against the present pontiff, well financed by the world's ultra-right.

But also the Eastern Churches, particularly the Orthodox Church of Russia, are more and more closing in on themselves, for fear of the "other," above all of the Muslim. In Russia, Putin is using religion to carry out his role as czar, and in a few years has made Russia the lighthouse of conservative thought and of the leaders of the extreme right, whom he generously finances. One of the emblematic figures of Russian fundamentalism is Aleksandr Dugin, who in 2018, from the terrace of Casa Pound in Rome, expounded his take on the status of the world: in a fearful fight between globalism and populism. Unfortunately, this phenomenon of fundamentalism is also taking hold in the other great churches of the West: Anglican, Lutheran, Calvinist, Methodist, and more.

One who understood this hold well was that great sage Tiziano Terzani: "In the conversations that I have had in the last two weeks with so many different Muslims in Pakistan," wrote Terzani in a letter from Quetta in his book *Lettere Contro La Guerra* (letters against the war),

> I have noticed a continuous reference to a sort of violence of which many now feel themselves the victims. The reason? The confrontation with the West. Right or wrong, many perceive globalization as an instrument of our "atheist and materialist civilization" which, precisely by means of the expansion of markets, is becoming ever more rich and more strong, to the detriment of their world.

Addressing this will be a long and difficult road, but it is one we must take, both personally and as a people. It is up to us, nonbelievers and believers of every religion alike, to enter onto this road.

But we have a splendid example in the life of one of our contemporaries, Pierre Claverie, a man who had to come out of his colonial cocoon to encounter the "other," the Muslim.

# 6

# A Contemporary Parable

## Coming out of the Colonial Cocoon

To me, Pierre Claverie is an exemplary figure, a member of the White Tribe who dedicated his entire life to the encounter with the "other," the Muslim. Pierre Claverie was born in 1938 at Bab El Oued, a district within the city of Algiers, to a family of French colonialists. The Claveries lived there for four generations.

So Pierre lived his childhood in the "colonial bell of glass," as he himself would later call it. In truth, although residing in an Arab and Muslim country, Pierre did not ever encounter the "other"! He grew up in his white community, very numerous in Algeria at the time. "I always wondered" he would relate in a conference at the Marseilles Club in 1995, "why, although being a Christian, hearing discourses on the love for one's neighbor, I had never heard that the Arab was my neighbor."

In 1957 Pierre was sent to France to attend the University of Grenoble. That was the precise moment when the Algerian Revolution broke out against France in favor of independence—a frightening war, with more than one million dead. It was a traumatic experience for Pierre, who, having grown up in a "colonial bubble," could not help but adopt the cause of France against the Algerian people. "Perhaps it was by my very ignorance of it, my denial of its existence," Pierre would later confess, "that, at the time, it seemed it was the 'other' who had injured me. It had exploded my closed world, which dissolved into violence, yet which continued to affirm its own existence."

In that time of total confusion Pierre frequented political groups of the right, but he quite soon realized that was not the road to take. Slowly the irruption of that "other" that he had never encountered demanded its own place, its own dignity, throwing him into a profound crisis. This crisis forced him to rethink his life and ask himself how "he had been able to live, and did live, as a Christian, without ever himself addressing the problem of the 'other.'"

This crisis was the beginning of his conversion, which he himself describes with these words: "The sudden appearance of the 'other,' the recognition of the 'other,' the adjustment to the 'other,' became for me an obsession." And he adds: "I said to myself: no more walls, no more borders, nor divisions. The 'other' must exist; otherwise we expose ourselves to violence, to exclusion, to rejection."

"It was probably this which gave rise to my religious vocation," he reflected. So it was that in 1959 he entered the Dominican order and for eight full years devoted himself to the study of theology. During these years his passion to encounter the "other" matured. And he understood not only that French Algeria was dead, but that it could not be defended, because it was built upon exclusion.

Algeria would obtain its independence in 1962. And with independence came the flight of the French Christian community.

With it also collapsed the colonial church in which Pierre had grown up.

"After independence, precisely because of it, I asked to return to Algeria," wrote Pierre, "to rediscover that world in which I had been born, but of which I had been ignorant. That was the beginning of my authentic personal adventure—a rebirth."

In 1967, Pierre landed in Algeria, so different from the Algeria in which he had been born. He dedicated himself completely to the study of the Arab and of Islam, and at the same time to the weaving of relationships with the Algerians. "It was necessary to enter, at all cost, ever more into learning the language, to begin to evaluate the *abyss that separates us*."

Pierre lived and worked at Algiers, in the shadow of the extraordinary figure of Cardinal Duval, whom the French reproached as "Mohamed Duval," because he had placed himself in the defense of the Algerians during the War of Independence. In 1973 Cardinal Duval named Pierre director of the Center of Language and Pastoral Studies. It was there that Pierre was able to encounter a great many Algerians, with whom he formed deep friendships. His passion was "discovering the other, living with the other, listening to him, letting himself be molded by the other. This did not mean losing one's own identity, rejecting one's own values, but conceiving a *pluralistic humanity*."

Reflecting on his life experience he arrived at the conclusion noted in the splendid biography by Adrien Candiard, *Pierre et Mohamed*:

> In my experience of enclosure, then of crisis, and of the emergence of the individual, I arrived at the personal conviction that there is *no humanity unless it's a*

*pluralistic one*, and that when we pretend to possess the truth (inside the Catholic Church we have experienced a sad history of this) or to speak in the name of truth, we fall into totalitarianism and into exclusion.

Pierre understood that even his own church, in its history over thousands of years, had fallen into this most grave error. It is enough to think of the Crusades against the Muslims (how they still weigh heavy on the relations between these two religions!), of the Inquisition, which sent so many people to burn at the stake, of the wars of religion (in which Catholics and Protestants butchered each other), and of the thousands of "witches" burned in Christian Europe.

## Pluralistic Humanity

It was this deep sense of humility that, for Pierre, made possible the encounter with the Algerians, who loved him as their own. In 1981 Pierre Claverie was named bishop of Oran, a city in the western part of the country. "Our job in Algeria is that of being deprived of our wealth, of our pretenses, and our sense of self-sufficiency. . . . We thank God when he restores his church to *simple humanity.*"

With independence, the church in Algeria had lost all its properties, which were confiscated by the state. It now became a church in service of the people, of the few Christians, but above all in the service of the Muslim majority. Pierre immersed himself in that world that he loved, hungry for genuine relationships. He was a man in search of the truth.

> Nobody possesses the truth; everyone searches for it; there are certainly objective truths, but which are

beyond us all and to which one cannot reach except by way of a long journey, and by piecing them together little by little, taking, from other cultures and from other human groups, that which others have attained to, and have searched for, in their own journey toward the truth.

Those were the profound convictions that motivated Pierre in his fifteen years as bishop of Oran. He was the bishop not only of the few Christians there, but even more than ever, the bishop of the Muslims. And he fashioned deep relations with the Islamists, from which bloomed friendships just as deep. Without ever proselytizing. "I am a believer; I believe there is a God. But I do not pretend to possess him, neither by way of Jesus who revealed him to me, nor by way of the dogmas of my faith. God *is not possessed*. The truth *is not possessed*; *I need the truth of others*."

But in 1992 the Islamic Salvation Front won the elections in Algeria; it was the beginning of a very heartrending period for the country. It was the ascent of radical Islam, the political Islam that proclaimed the establishment of an Islamic republic.

Pierre understood immediately the danger inherent in the "sanctification of power or politics, making of it the application of a divine model." For him, Christianity, too, over the course of history, had suffered from a similar amalgamation of religion and politics. And in response he sought to help all Christians and Muslims to reflect on the implications. He wrote in the daily newspapers; he spoke on television; the bishop of Oran became a public personage.

On January 11, 1992, the Algerian president, Bendjedid Chadli, "resigned" under pressure from the army, which then took power into its own hands. On March 4, the Islamic

Salvation Front was dissolved and its members were arrested and deported to concentration camps in the Sahara. These brutal measures did nothing but augment the popularity of armed Islamic groups responsible for a series of assassinations of intellectuals, artists, and others.

It was the beginning of a ruthless war between the military and the fundamentalists. More than fifty thousand persons—women, children, intellectuals, imams, soldiers, rebels—perished in that fratricidal conflict.

The fundamentalists had warned all foreigners, including the religious, to leave the country, threatening them with death. Many went. But many remained, ready to pay with their lives. "Since I am bishop of a church in Algeria, I will remain," affirmed Pierre. "The blood of the one side and of the other is mixed in violence. Jesus placed himself on these fracture lines of humanity. That is where he died. It is the meaning of the crucifixion."

Pierre remained because he believed in a pluralistic Algeria, as did a majority of the Algerian people.

> We are not the first to face violence and death with our bare hands and only the force of our convictions. And we are not even alone. In the moments in which we could be tempted to flee . . . we must listen to the voice of those who have faced death with the offer of their own lives, to testify to their faith in the omnipotence of love and of life!

From May 1994 to August 1996, at least nineteen religious paid with their lives for their decision to remain at the side of the Algerian people. It is an extraordinary story related in the book *Our Death Does Not Belong to Us*. The most widely known are the seven monks of Tibhirine with their prior, Christian de Chergé, who left us an extraordinary spiritual testament:

> If it should happen to me someday (and it could be today) that I should be victim of the terrorism that seems to want to involve all foreigners who live in Algeria, I would want my community, my church, my family, to remember that my life was *donated* to God and to this country.

And it concludes:

> And you too, friend of the last minute who will not have known what it was that you were doing. Yes, for you, too, I want this *grace*, and this *good-bye*[1] awaiting you. And that it may be given us to see each other again, as good thieves, in paradise,[2] if it please God, our Father, the Father of both of us. Amen! *Inshallah*."[3]

The last of the Catholic religious of the country to be killed was Pierre Claverie, on August 1, 1996, together with Mohamed Bouchikhi. Pierre knew well that he was in the crosshairs of the fundamentalists. He was a public figure who took

---

[1] Translator's note: The Italian for "goodbye," *addio* (as well as the French *adieu*), as used here, presents a virtual play on words that is fairly untranslatable into English, as it is a combination of two words (*a* and *dio*) meaning, literally, both "goodbye," and "to God," that is, the "play on words" used by de Chergé.

[2] Translator's note: One of the last words of Jesus on the cross was to the good thief: "Today you will be with me in Paradise" (Lk 23:43).

[3] Translator's note: Arabic, which, according to commonly available sources, can be translated as "if God wills it" or "God willing."

public positions on the problems of the country in the daily newspapers and on television. At the end of July 1996 he set out for Algiers, by plane, for an important meeting.

He arrived at the Algiers airport on August 1, where he found Mohamed Bouchikhi, a good friend, a young man of twenty-one years, waiting for him. Mohamed often accompanied him on this travels in Algiers, driving him around. "I know that Pierre will die," Mohamed had written in his notebook. "And I too know very well that I will be threatened as he will, accompanying him everywhere. But if I die with Pierre, in my pockets they will find a little notebook in which I note my thoughts and my prayers."

And Mohamed concluded his reflection with the common prayer of Muslims: "In the name of God, the Merciful, the Compassionate."

As Pierre got off the plane, Mohamed welcomed him and accompanied him to the car as they prepared to drive home—a car in which the fundamentalists had placed a bomb. As they entered the vehicle and Mohamed turned on the light, the bomb tore Pierre and Mohamed apart. Christian blood and Muslim blood were mixed together.

"If only, in the Algerian crisis," Pierre had written,

> after this moment of violence and deep fractures in society, but also in religion and identity, the concept would then arrive that *the other has the right to exist*, that he carries a truth and is to be respected, then we shall not have undergone in vain the dangers to which we are now exposed.

# 7

# . . . To You, the Young

The example of Pierre Claverie is a splendid one, showing how a French colonialist in Algeria succeeded in coming out from the "colonial bubble" in which he had lived to encounter the "other," the Muslim. Today this road he traveled is one the White Tribe is obliged to travel, too—we must come out from the "colonial bubble" to encounter the "other."

I have written this open letter during the time of the pandemic, which has allowed me a series of reflections on our system—the bitter fruit of five centuries of colonialism and of exploitation of the peoples of the earth, which continue to this day.

The harm that the White Tribe has done is so evident that only cynics could deny it. But the recognition of the harm done must push the White Tribe to abandon a road of death to begin on another bringing the fruits of justice for everyone. And if it is for the older generation to recognize the harm done, it will be up to you, the young, to find new roads.

I am now eighty-three years old, years lived in radical conditions for the impoverished of the planet, who have converted me, pulling me out from the "colonial bubble" in which I, too, had lived. To you, the young, I confess that my generation will be among those most cursed at in human history because no other generation has so gravely violated and exploited the planet.

I ask pardon of you, the young, because we leave you a world gravely ill, and it will be up to your generation to radically rethink our financial, economic, and military systems, which oppress billions of people and suffocate the planet, causing the grave ecological crisis that oppresses us.

You are not the *future* of the world (even if everyone tells you that you are); you are the only *present* we have to save *Homo sapiens*, together with the earth. But to make this happen, you too must come out of the "cocoon." It will be a demanding process that will require a rereading of our history, starting with the impoverished themselves, and of the system of death in which we live. But above all it will require the will to encounter the "other," the different, the impoverished, to understand how they read reality.

Nobody possesses the truth; it is sought together, above all sought with those impoverished by the system. It is the path that the great pedagogue Father Lorenzo Milani[1] took to reread Italian history together with his boys of Barbiana. "They presented us [in 1936] with the Empire as the glory

---

[1] Translator's note: Father Lorenzo Milani, 1923–67, grew up and matured during the rule of Mussolini and World War II. Ordained a Catholic priest in 1947 in the diocese of Florence, in 1954 he was assigned to a parish in a tiny mountain town, Barbiana, where he established a school for boys. From there he became controversial within the church, with the Vatican's Holy Office removing his book *Pastoral Experiences* from circulation as "inopportune." He was later charged criminally over his open letter written to military chaplains concerning conscientious objection.

of the Fatherland!" he wrote in his *Lettera Ai Giudici* (letter to the judges).

> I was thirteen years old, I believe. I jumped for joy for the Fatherland. Our teachers forgot to tell us that the Ethiopians were better than we were. That we went to burn their huts with their women and their children inside, when they had done exactly nothing to us. That vile school, whether on purpose or not I do not know, was preparing the horrors of three years later. It was preparing millions of obedient soldiers. Obedient to the orders of Mussolini. Or rather, to be more precise, obedient to the orders of Hitler. Fifty million dead.

This was what led Father Milani to address his boys and the young people of Italy with these hard words:

> Have the courage to tell young people that they are all sovereigns, that obedience is no longer a virtue but the most insidious of temptations, that they should not think they can use it as a shield before men or before God, that they should consider themselves—each one of them—solely responsible for everything

These are words that should be carved into the walls of all schools, and, above all, in all of your young minds.

✧✧✧

This is why I am writing to you—you who are young.

You have a unique and fundamental role in this historic moment when the survival of human life on this planet is itself at stake.

In your youth, do not take the side of that camp which has already raised the white flag of surrender, thinking that there is nothing you can do; you have, in reality, an enormous power. Do not bend to this system, but dedicate yourself to changing it. Do not let yourself be paralyzed with fear, but respond with courage. Do not stand in silence, but rise up and out of your home, united with others, and descend on the public square to demand that the powerful change paths.

In your youth be a little star in this world of darkness and follow a dream, a beautiful dream, the dream of a more just and fraternal world: "Have a beautiful dream; follow only a dream, the dream of all life," wrote Ezechiel Ramin, a Comboni missionary, killed at thirty-three for his work on behalf of the peasant farmers and the Indigenous peoples of the Amazon.

And I assure you that a life lived cultivating the dream of making the whole of humanity happy is beautiful. And it is enchanting when you live it for the "other," for the common good, for a more fraternal world. I admit, too, that in my life, given and donated to the impoverished, to the marginalized, I have experienced the joy of life. It is precisely this which Jesus of Nazareth expressed in his extraordinary words: "Those who want to save their life will lose it, and those who lose their life for my sake will find it [Matt 16:25]."

Have the courage to be indignant, to rethink, and to reinvent all, to make a more human world flower and bloom. Now it is your turn, you the young, to humanize mankind!